HUMAN & MACHINE
PERCEPTION

Communication, Interaction, and Integration

HUMAN & MACHINE
PERCEPTION
Communication, Interaction, and Integration

Santa Caterina di Pittinuri, Oristano, Italy
September 6–9, 2004

EDITORS

SERGIO VITULANO
Dipartimento di Scienze Mediche e Internistiche, Università di Cagliari
Policlinico Universitario, Monserrato, 09042 Cagliari, Italy

VITO DI GESÙ
Dipartimento di Matematica ed Applicazioni, Università Di Palermo
Via Archirafi 34, 90123 Palermo, Italy

VIRGINIO CANTONI * ROBERTO MARMO * ALESSANDRA SETTI
Dipartimento Informatica, e Sistemistica, Università di Pavia, via Ferrata 1
27100 Pavia, Italy

World Scientific

NEW JERSEY • LONDON • SINGAPORE • BEIJING • SHANGHAI • HONG KONG • TAIPEI • CHENNAI

Published by

World Scientific Publishing Co. Pte. Ltd.

5 Toh Tuck Link, Singapore 596224

USA office: 27 Warren Street, Suite 401-402, Hackensack, NJ 07601

UK office: 57 Shelton Street, Covent Garden, London WC2H 9HE

British Library Cataloguing-in-Publication Data
A catalogue record for this book is available from the British Library.

ISBN-13 978-981-238-431-7
ISBN-10 981-238-431-6

Printed in Singapore

PREFACE

The following are the proceedings of the Sixth International Workshop on Human and Machine Perception held in Santa Caterina di Pittinuri (Oristano), Italy, on September 06-09, 2004, under the auspices of the following Institutions: the Italian Ministry of the University and the Researches, the University of Cagliari, the Pavia University, and the Inter-Department Centers of Cognitive Sciences of Palermo University.

A broad spectrum of topics are covered in this series, ranging from computer perception to psychology and physiology of perception. The theme of this workshop on Human and Machine Perception was focused on *Communication, Interaction and Integration*. As in the past editions the final goal has been the analysis and the comparison of biological and artificial solutions.

The focus of the lectures has been on presenting the state-of-the-art and outlining open questions. In particular, they sought to stress links, suggesting possible synergies between the different cultural areas. The panel discussion has been conceived as a forum for an open debate, briefly introduced by each panelist, and mainly aimed at deeper investigation of the different approaches to perception and strictly related topics. The panelists were asked to prepare a few statements on hot-points as a guide for discussion. These statements were delivered to the participants together with the final program, for a more qualified discussion.

The number of participants to the workshop was limited to 70. Besides the 8 invited lecturers and panelists, more participants were admitted. Priority for these positions was given to young researchers who made significant contributions to the open discussions. Both the lectures and the contents of the panel discussions are included in these proceedings.

The workshop structure consisted of three modules each of one organized in four general talks. The first one, *Representing and coding for communication*, was grounded on general talks and a panel discussion to give the foundations. The second one, *Exploration, visualization and discovering in very large data set*, was focused on methodologies for data mining, classification and recognition. The third one, *Information exchange: Machine versus Machine,* was dedicated to the communication and interaction of hybrid complex systems.

In this edition we included, for the second time in the series, also a few solicited presentations from the audience.

The description of both natural and artificial structures and basic approaches represents a natural starting point for a workshop which intends to analyze the processes of systems communication, interaction and integration from different viewpoints. The lectures were organized by alternating the functional descriptions of natural and artificial information management and decision making related to perception, learning, knowledge acquisition and storage. Further inquiries concern the human ability to exploit spatial information for reasoning and communication purposes and the new technologies and facilities on this field.

Representing and coding for communication intends to addressed and to explore basic references for communication processes that allow natural or/and artificial systems to exchange knowledge and information to achieve a smart situated behaviour. Tools and modalities (languages, protocols, coding schemes, ect.) for handling perceptual information are discussed and compared. Advances in technology lead towards communications that are often mediated by computers and networks.

Exploration and discovering in very large dataset explores how multimedia technology supplies a new way of gaining understanding into large data structures, allowing the user to gain insight into the process under investigation. Data-mining provides a new tool consisting of automatic discovering of patterns, changes, correlations and anomalies through an interactive display and analysis of data up to the elicitation of information and knowledge. Progress in statistics and data analysis are also shown in relation with data retrieving and discovering.

Information exchange: machine versus machine is addressed to information exchange among the living and how human being and machines may interact for improving performances and/or behavior. In particular, the usability of a given multi-media interface, in terms of performance interface evaluation, is investigated. Moreover, how machines exchange information, learn by experimenting, and improve their performances is discussed. Modalities of interaction among distributed and heterogeneous systems, coordination in multi-agent systems, control strategies and suitable hierarchies are compared.

The workshop dealt with most of these problems and the results of the presentations and discussions are herewith included even if the chapters of the book vary somewhat from the scheduled program, to take care of the positions that emerged from the debates and to the audience reactions.

Acknowledgements

The workshop, and thus indirectly this book, was made possible through the generous financial support of the universities involved, and the research organizations that are listed separately. Their support is gratefully acknowledged.

In particular we would like to thank Roberto Marmo and Alessandra Setti for the completion of this volume. We are also grateful for the assistance offered by World Scientific for the preparation of this volume.

Virginio Cantoni, Vito Di Gesù, Sergio Vitulano

SPONSORING INSTITUTIONS

The following institutions are gratefully acknowledged for their contributions and support to the Workshop:

- MURST, Ministero dell'Università e della Ricerca Scientifica e Tecnologica, Italy
- Dottorato di Ricerca in Tecnologie Biomediche Applicate alle Scienze odontostomatologiche, Seconda Università di Napoli, Italy
- Dottorato di ricerca in Alimenti e Salute: Biotecnologie e Metodologie Applicate alla Fisiopatologia Digestiva, Seconda Università di Napoli, Italy
- Università di Cagliari, Italy
- Università di Pavia, Italy
- Università di Palermo, Italy
- Provincia di Cagliari, Italy

CONTENTS

INFORMATION EXCHANGE: MACHINE VERSUS MACHINE

ONE EYE, TWO EYES... HOW MANY EYES?
NOTES AND REFLECTIONS ON VISION SYSTEMS FOR
MOBILE ROBOTICS[*]

GIOVANNI ADORNI

Dipartimento di Informatica, Sistemistica e Telematica,
Università di Genova,
Via all'Opera Pia 13,
16145 Genoa, Italy
E-mail: adorni@unige.it

STEFANO CAGNONI, MONICA MORDONINI

Dipartimento di Ingegneria dell'Informazione,
Università di Parma,
Parco Area delle Scienze 181a,
43100 Parma, Italy
E-mail: {cagnoni,monica}@ce.unipr.it

In this chapter we discuss some issues on mobile robot perception from the point of view of the structure of vision systems. Through some experiences and results from research projects we will approach the problem from the point of view of purposive vision, with particular regard to less conventional sensors and systems, such as omnidirectional and hybrid systems.

1. Introduction

Differentiation of living beings is the most outstanding result of million of years of natural evolution. The main characterizing feature of Darwinian evolutionary processes is having the fitness of an individual, with respect to the surrounding environment and to performing the actions required to survive in it, as both their goal and driving force. As a result, each species has developed its own specialized *apparatus*, which maximize performance in its specific environment. Sensory and locomotory systems are probably the ones for which species differentiation is most immediately evident.

[*] This work was partially supported by ASI (Italian Space Agency) within the grants "Coordination of the cluster Robotic Vision" and "Hybrid Vision System for Long Range Rovering", and by ENEA (National Institute for Alternative Energy) within the grant "Sensori Intelligenti".

For many living beings, among sensory systems, the vision system is the richest source of information which is used to realize where they are and what is around them, in order to plan what their immediate goal should be and what sequence of actions should be performed to reach it. A basic taxonomy of vision systems in animal species can be based, firstly, on the number of sensitive elements by which an eye is composed and on the number of eyes; secondly, on features such as their field of view and sensitivity to light or colour.

Virtually all vertebrates, along with some invertebrates such as molluscs, medusas and worms, have simple eyes, similar to humans'. Obviously, despite their similar physical structure, their performance generally differs, according to the environmental conditions in which they are expected to operate.

For instance, cats, bats, owls, which usually act in dark environments, if not exclusively at night-time, have only rods, more sensitive and numerous than in human eyes, to obtain high sensitivity to light. In dolphins' eyes, as well, there are 7000 times as many rods as in humans, to cope with limited underwater lighting.

Fish eyes have usually a flat cornea and a spherical, non-deformable crystalline lens, to improve sight in the near field of view. On the other hand, birds' eyes are elongated in antero-posterior direction to produce larger images of distant objects.

Among invertebrates, one of arthropods' peculiar features is having composite eyes, made up of many (up to thousands) simple eyes. The final image which they perceive is formed as apposition or superposition of the single images which are perceived by the simple eyes.

Similarly to what has been happening in natural evolution through million of years, the choices made by designers of vision systems for mobile robots are mainly influenced by the tasks which the robots, on which such systems are going to be mounted, are expected to perform. In computer vision, the purposive vision approach aims at solving problems encountered in dealing with complex tasks or environments by identifying the goal of the task; this simplifies design by making explicit just that piece of information that is needed to achieve such a goal. As a matter of fact, mobile robotics is probably the field in which the purposive vision paradigm has been applied most frequently. Mobile robotics applications actually require that task-specific information be selected from the usually huge amount available, to satisfy the constraints of real-time or just-in-time processing imposed by the dynamic environments in which mobile robotics tasks are usually performed.

In designing robot vision systems the main degrees of freedom available to the designer are the same peculiarities that distinguish biological vision systems, namely the number of sensors and some of their features, of which the width of the field of view and the related parameters of distortion and resolution are perhaps the most relevant. Therefore, also in the case of robotic vision systems, a similar taxonomy to the one reported above for natural vision systems can be applied.

In this chapter, we aim at discussing the task of designing robot vision systems according to such a taxonomy and from the point of view of purposive vision applications. The chapter reviews examples of applications or preliminary experiences we developed in previous research projects, highlighting the task-oriented motivation of design, and discussing the results that such systems can achieve.

We will consider the case of single-sensor systems, as opposed to multi-sensor ones. As regards sensor types, we will consider traditional pin-hole and omnidirectional sensors in single or multi-sensor configurations. Particular attention will be given to the design of omnidirectional and hybrid omnidirectional/pin-hole systems.

2. Single-sensor Systems

Up to a few years ago, most computer vision applications relied on single-sensor systems. However, the choice very often did not depend on an objective evaluation of the specifications on the design of the vision system, but mostly on constraints imposed by the computation power that was available. As processor power increases, along with sensor technology, it is possible to design computer vision applications which are more and more complex, both intrinsically and from the point of view of the sensors by which information is acquired. Mobile robotics applications, in particular, have become more and more reliant on heterogeneous sensory systems (cameras, ultrasonic sensors, laser scanners, etc.), in which even the vision system is often made up of multiple, homogeneous or heterogeneous, components.

In the far-from-complete review of vision sensors made by this chapter, attention is principally focused onto multi-sensor vision systems. Therefore, discussion of single-sensor system will be limited to describing their essential features, considering them mainly as basic components of more complex systems. Also, since the main focus of this chapter is on less conventional sensor design, in describing conventional cameras we will limit our discussion to a very concise review of the main features which affect performance of mobile robot vision systems. In particular we will focus on the features which distinguish conventional from omnidirectional sensors, discussing the latter more amply, even if, also in their case, with the aim of introducing them as components of multi-sensor systems.

2.1. Conventional Cameras

Conventional cameras use the classic pin-hole principle, by which objects in a scene are projected onto a planar sensor after being focused on it by a lens, or simply after the light rays which they reflect pass through a tiny hole.

If the size and resolution of the sensor are set, the field of view of such a system is inversely dependent on the focal distance, i.e. the distance between the lens (hole) and the sensor onto which the image is projected. Conversely, the resolution of the image which can be obtained increases with the focal distance, since a smaller scene is projected onto the same sensitive area.

Images acquired by conventional cameras are affected by two kinds of distortions: perspective effects and deformations that derive from the shape of the lens through which the scene is observed. Both kinds of distortion hamper direct measures, since distances in pixel are not proportional to actual distances in the real world.

In mobile robotics applications, being able to reconstruct the surrounding scene with high accuracy is a critical task in navigation, especially as obstacle detection and motion planning are concerned.

After introducing omnidirectional sensors in the next section, we introduce the Inverse Perspective Transform (IPT) as a general tool to, firstly, compensate for the classical perspective distortion in pin-hole images and, more generally, to compensate for any measurable distortion in images acquired by any sort of vision sensor. IPT can be effectively used to detect obstacles in mobile robotics application based on stereo vision systems, as shown in Section 3.2.

2.2. Omnidirectional Cameras

Being able to see behind one's shoulders has probably been one of the most desirable supernatural faculties for humans (possibly the most desirable after being able to fly), resulting in several mythological creatures, such as Janus, the divinity with two faces, and Argus Panoptes, the giant with a hundred eyes.

In applications involving dynamic environments such as mobile robotics, widening the field of view is of major importance, to be able to enhance awareness about what is happening in the surroundings and to obviate the need for active cameras, that require complex control strategies. In this section we will consider a particular class of omnidirectional sensors, catadioptric sensors, which consist of a conventional camera that acquires the image reflected on a convex mirror.

Catadioptric omnidirectional sensors suffer from two main limitations. The most relevant one is that the near field, which is the least distorted part of the image, is partially obstructed by the reflection of the camera on the mirror. A further limitation is that the accumulation of camera and system distortions makes it quite difficult either to find the resulting distortion law and to compensate for it, or to design a mirror profile that can achieve a good trade-off between width of the field of view, image resolution and distortion (see [5] for a discussion of the problem). To reduce this effect, mirrors that produce a non-distorted image of a reference plane have been recently described [13,16].

Omnidirectional systems are therefore very efficient as concerns detection of target position, but critical from the point of view of the accuracy with which the target is detected. For these reasons, either the omnidirectional vision sensor has been integrated with a different kind of sensor, to make object detection and robot self-localization more precise and robust (see, for example [9,12,15,19], or arrays of omnidirectional sensors have been used to implement triangulation algorithms [20]. In the following section we discuss the problem of designing omnidirectional systems from the point of view of mobile robotics applications.

2.2.1. *Design of catadioptric omnidirectional systems*

One of the most important issues in designing a catadioptric omnidirectional vision system is choosing the geometry of the reflecting surface of the mirror [14]. Different mirror profiles have been proposed in literature [21].

In particular, adopting the solution proposed by [13] one can design a mirror which preserves the geometry of a plane perpendicular to the axis of symmetry of the reflecting surface, i.e., an isometric mirror: the mirror acts as a computational sensor, capable of providing distortion-free images automatically, thus eliminating the need for further processing, if the distortion caused by the camera lens is neglected. Other researchers propose the use of multi-part mirrors [8], composed of a spherical mirror providing better resolution in the proximity of the robot to accurately localize significant features in the environment, merged with a conic mirror that extends the field of view of the system, to perceive objects at a greater distance at the price of a loss in resolution. This composite mirror shape permits to image objects that are closer to the sensor with respect to classical off-the-shelf conical mirrors that are often used to achieve omnidirectional vision. This design has been suggested by the requirements of RoboCup,[a] in which robots need to see the ball up to the point at which they touch it.

---

[a] Visit http://www.robocup.org for information on the RoboCup robot soccer competition.

Obviously, to design the profile of a mirror it is always necessary to first define the requirements for the particular application for which the catadioptric vision system is meant; thus a general rule for generating the optimum mirror profile does not exist. For example, a vision system which is meant only for obstacle avoidance probably does not require that the robot recognize very distant objects; the opposite is true for a localization system which relies on the recognition of significant features distributed on the walls or extracted from the surrounding environment [9]. Once the requirements for a particular application have been specified, to design a mirror profile with the desired characteristics, a differential equation needs to be solved, which can be inferred by applying the laws of linear optics. The following specifications, suggested by considerations related with both the optics and the mechanics of the system, are to be met in mobile robot vision systems:

1. minimizing encumbrance and weight of the mirror by minimizing its radius. If one considers that the whole vision system is typically made up of a camera and a transparent cylinder holding the mirror, by reducing the mirror weight (and, if possible, the cylinder height) the mechanical stability of the whole system is increased. Notice also that, for a given focal length of the camera, decreasing the radius of the mirror also requires that the distance between the camera and the reflecting surface be decreased as well as, consequently, the height of the support;

2. designing profiles which reduce the area of the image containing useless information, e.g., the reflection of the robot on the mirror;

3. radially extending the field of view up to where relevant information can be still extracted;

4. keeping the resolution of the most relevant part of the image as high as possible, to provide the clearest possible view of the objects that lie close to it and require that the robot take strictly real-time decisions in dealing with them.

The rationale behind these basic requirements is clear if one observes Figure 1, in which a cheap but clearly non-optimal catadioptric surface (the convex face of a ladle!) has been used to acquire an omnidirectional view of a RoboCup field, in which a ball is placed at a distance of 1 *m* from the sensor.

In such an image, the most evident problems are:

1. poor resolution already at a relatively short distance: the ball is hardly visible, despite being at a distance of about 1 meter;

2. extension of the field of view beyond the area of interest: useless low-resolution information (very distant objects) is visible;

3. the image region occupied by the reflection of the robot body on the mirror is very large.

Figure 1. A 'home-made' omnidirectional sensor obtained using a kitchen ladle.

According to the above-mentioned guidelines, we have designed a mirror which is very similar to the one in Figure 2. The mirror is obtained as a revolution surface by revolving the profile around the z-axis, it has a radius of 5 cm and it is about 2.69 cm high.

The profile can be decomposed in two sections: the first section (from point A to point B) can be modeled as an arc of circumference, while the second section (from point B to point C) is a straight line. The tangent to the circumference in point B has the same slope as the straight line, preserving the continuity in the first order derivative. Observing the resulting surface (see Figure 3), it is straightforward to see that it is composed by a conic mirror jointed to an "almost spherical" mirror. On one hand, the property of the conic part to reflect objects which are far from the robot is very useful to detect objects of interest (other robots, openings, signs on walls, etc.). Obviously, resolution decreases with object distance from the robot, allowing only for an approximate perception of the distance of interesting features. However, if focusing on a particular feature

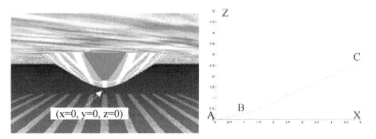

Figure 2. Catadioptric omnidirectional sensor for mobile robotics applications and its generating profile.

is needed, the system provides sufficient information for the robot to move towards it, until it can perceive its geometric properties (position and shape) more accurately. On the other hand, the property of the spherical part to reflect close objects with a higher resolution is well suited for obstacle detection and avoidance.

As regards reducing the extension of the image region containing useless information, since this area is situated in the center of the image and corresponds to the reflection of the camera onto the central part of the mirror, one can introduce a discontinuity in the gradient of the revolution surface in correspondence of point $(x=0, y=0, z=0)$. In Figure 3 it can be easily seen that, since the first order derivative of the curve in correspondence of $(x=0, z=0)$ is not equal to zero, the resulting revolution surface will have a discontinuity in $(x=0, y=0, z=0)$. By varying the slope of the tangent in such a point one can obtain different revolution surfaces. This means that a distortion is introduced in the reflected image, such that the central area which contains useless information is significantly shrunk.

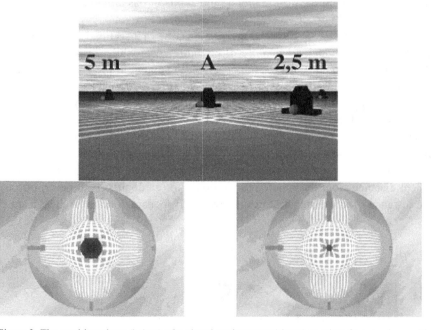

Figure 3. The resulting views (below) of a virtual environment (above) as taken from a mirror with no discontinuities (left) and a mirror with a discontinuous profile in the point $(x=0, y=0, z=0)$ (right).

2.2.2. *Inverse Perspective Transform*

While distortions due to lens shape can be completely removed if the lens model and its corresponding parameters are known or if a proper empirical calibration using a reference shape is performed, perspective effect removal from a single view is possible only with respect to an arbitrary chosen plane. Everything that lies on such a plane will be reconstructed as seen in an orthogonal projection onto the plane, i.e., with no perspective distortion. The problem can therefore be formalized as that of finding a function $P_{x,y} = C(I_{i,j})$ that maps each pixel in the image $I_{i,j}$ onto the corresponding point $P_{x,y}$ of a new image P (with coordinates x,y) that represents an orthogonal projection onto the reference plane. Therefore, limiting one's interest to objects lying on the reference plane, it is possible to reason on the scene observing it with no distortions, at least on the plane level. The most appealing feature, in this case, is that a direct-proportionality relationship between distances in the reconstructed image and in the real world can be obtained, which is a fundamental requirement for geometrical reasoning. This transformation is often referred to as Inverse Perspective Transform (IPT) [1,17,18], since perspective-effect removal is the most common aim with which it is performed, even if it actually represents only one of the problems for which it provides a solution. For any different plane, one such function must be computed that differs from any other. Everything that does not lie on the reference plane is affected by a distortion that depends on its distance from the plane and on its position with respect to the camera.

If all parameters related to the geometry of the acquisition systems and to the distortions introduced by the camera were known, the derivation of C could be straightforward. However, this is not always the case, most often because of the lack of an exact model of camera distortion. However, it is often possible to effectively (and efficiently) derive C empirically using proper calibration algorithms. An empirical derivation of C through a point-to-point mapping between the actual view and the transformed one is virtually possible for any kind of cameras.

We will consider here the problem of computing C_o, the generalization of the IPT for a catadioptric omnidirectional sensor. In this case, the problem is complicated by the non-planar profile of the mirror; on the other hand, the circular symmetry of the device provides the opportunity of dramatically simplifying such a procedure.

If the reflecting surface were perfectly manufactured, it would be sufficient to compute just the restriction of C_o along one radius of the mirror projection on the image plane to compute the whole function. However, possible manufacturing flaws may affect both shape and surface smoothness of the mirror. In addition to singularities that do not affect sensor symmetry and can be included in the radial model of the mirror (caused, for example, by the joint between two differently shaped surfaces, as discussed before), a few other minor isolated flaws can be found scattered over the surface. Similar considerations can be made regarding the lens through which the image reflected on the mirror is captured by the camera.

To account for all sorts of distortions an empirical derivation of C_0 based on an appropriate sampling of the function in the image space can be made. Choosing such a procedure to compute C_0 permits to include also the lens model into the mapping function.

The basic principle by which C_0 can be derived empirically is to consider a set of equally-spaced radii, along each of which values of C_0 are computed for a set of uniformly-sampled points for which the relative position with respect to the sensor is known exactly. This produces a polar grid of points for which the values of C_0 are known.

To compute the function for a generic point P located anywhere in the field of view of the sensor, an interpolation can be made between the set of points among which P is located. The number of data-points (interpolation nodes) needed to achieve sufficient accuracy depends mainly on the mirror profile and on the mirror surface quality.

This calibration process can be automated, especially in the presence of well manufactured mirrors, by automatically detecting relevant points. To do so, a simple pattern consisting of a white stripe with a set of aligned black squares superimposed on it can be used, as shown in Figure 4.

The reference data-points, to be used as nodes for the grid, are extracted by automatically detecting the squares in a set of one or more images grabbed turning the robot around the vertical axis of the sensor. Doing so the reference pattern is reflected by different mirror portions in each image.

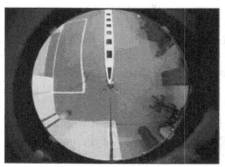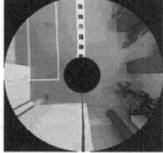

Figure 4. An example of IPT transformation of an image acquired by an omnidirectional camera.

If distances between the shapes forming the pattern are known exactly, the only requirement is that one of the shapes, at known distance, be distinguishable (e.g., by its colour) from the others. The shape should be possibly located within the highest-resolution area of the sensor. This makes it possible to use the reference shape as a landmark to automatically measure the distance from the camera of every shape on the reference plane, while removing the need to accurately position the robot at a predefined distance from the pattern, which could be a further source of calibration errors.

Operatively, in the first step of the automatic calibration process, the white stripe, along with the centres of the reference shape, are easily detected. These reference points are inserted into the set of samples on which interpolation is then performed. The process can be repeated for different headings of the robot, simply turning the robot around its central symmetry axis. In the second step, interpolation is performed to compute the function C_0 from the point set extracted as described. A look-up table that associates each pair of coordinates in the IPT-transformed image to a pair of coordinates in the original image can thus be computed. This calibration process is fast and provides good results, as shown in Figure 4.

The IPT plays an important role in several applications in which finding a relevant reference plane is easy. This is true for most indoor Mobile Service Robotics applications (such as surveillance of banks and warehouses, transportation of goods, escort for people at exhibitions and museums, etc.), since most objects which the robot observes and with which it interacts lie in fact on the same plane surface of the floor on which the robot is moving. For the same reason, the transform can be effectively used also in traditional fixed-camera surveillance systems.

3. Multi-sensor Systems

In considering vision systems which rely on the use of more than one sensor, a first distinction between two broad categories of systems can be made.

The first category comprises those systems in which the presence of many sensors simply aims at achieving an extension of the field of view or, more in general, an extension of the quantity of information which can be acquired: information acquired by each sensor is usually (pre-)processed independently, and only at a later stage are results of independent processing jointly evaluated. The second category, on the contrary, involves those systems, such as stereo systems, in which data acquired by one sensor is typically relevant to the application only if processed concurrently with data coming from the other sensors. In the following sections we will provide examples of multi-sensor systems belonging to the above-mentioned categories, with particular regard to the vision system of a robot goal-keeper designed to compete in the RoboCup middle-size league, and to a hybrid vision system with stereo capabilities which is being tested for both robotics and surveillance applications.

3.1. *Conventional Multi-camera Systems*

In several applications, in which accurate and fast action is required from a mobile robot, there is the need for vision systems which provide, at the same time, wide field of view, high resolution and limited distortion. In practical terms, this means offering the opportunity to focus onto the objects of interests instantaneously, to analyse them in details, and to be able to dedicate as much computation power as possible to image processing and understanding algorithm by limiting the cost of camera control strategies.

Such goals can be achieved by multi-camera system, based on conventional sensors, in which the field of view of each of the N sensors covers about $1/N^{th}$ of the scene of interest. This is the case, for example, of the vision sensor of Galavrón, the robot goal-keeper [4] we designed to compete in the RoboCup middle-size league.

Figure 5 shows the goal-keeper. The robot vision system is based on two wide-angle cameras, that allow the visual field to be more than 180° wide. The cameras are placed on top of the goalie. The fields of view of the two cameras, each of which extends by about 70° vertically and by about 110° horizontally, overlap in a region about 20° wide which corresponds to the centre of the zone that lies immediately in front of the robot. As anticipated, to simplify camera control and co-ordination as much as possible, the two cameras are connected to two frame grabbers, which can be operated independently of each other. It is crucial for goal-keeper operation that no frame in which the ball is visible be lost.

 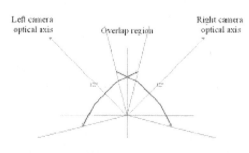

Figure 5. The robot goal-keeper Galavrón and the field of view of its vision system.

An extremely simple acquisition strategy can be implemented as follows: when the ball cannot be detected by either of the two cameras, the camera from which the image is acquired is switched at each new frame acquisition. When the ball is detected by one of the two cameras the image is acquired from that camera until it enters the overlap region. At that point the other camera is switched on for acquisition. Such a strategy can be easily extended to systems having more than two sensors.

Absolute localization and repositioning are based on vision, too. Each time the ball is not visible the goalie enters the repositioning mode, and uses the front line of the goal-keeper area to determine its location and to reposition itself in the middle of the area just in front of the goal. To do so, an efficient algorithm is used, based on a comparison between the orientation and intercept point of the lines delimiting the goal-keeper area, as acquired by the left and the right camera, as shown in Figure 6.

To detect lines, the first step which is performed is colour segmentation of the image, followed by edge detection. Only the edges of the white areas are then transformed into the Hough domain [11], to allow for an easy computation of the parameters of the line equation.

Once the parameters are known and the intersection between the visible lines is detected, the following parameters:

1. coordinates of goal-keeper area vertices;
2. position of goal relative to the robot;
3. distance from goal

are used to detect one of 24 possible positions, which have been previously identified, for each of which a different closed-form solution to the localization problem, computed on such parameters, exists.

3.2. *Conventional Stereo Systems*

Stereo vision is usually obtained by two cameras slightly displaced from each other, thus being characterised by having a widely overlapping field of view, or through the acquisition of two images from a single sensor that can move to simulate the availability of two cameras displaced as above. The sensors can be traditional cameras or even omnidirectional sensors [10].

The displacement of the two cameras generates two images of the same scene, taken from two different points of view. By comparing the two images it is therefore possible to compute stereo disparity and, from such data and from knowledge of the geometry of the acquisition system, to infer some three-dimensional properties of the objects in the scene.

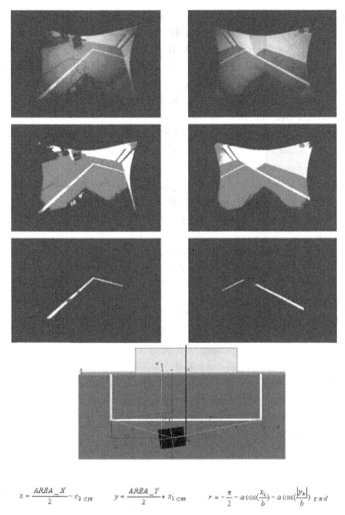

$$x = \frac{AREA\_X}{2} - c_{2\,cm} \qquad y = \frac{AREA\_Y}{2} + x_{1\,cm} \qquad r = -\frac{\pi}{2} - a\cos(\frac{x_1}{b}) - a\cos(\frac{|y_a|}{b})\;_{rad}$$

Figure 6. Above, from top: image acquisition, color segmentation, line detection. Below: one of the 24 possible solutions to the localization problem.

3.2.1. *Computing stereo disparity*

Figure 7 shows a general case study for stereo systems: the same point P is observed from two points of view O1 and O2. Stereo disparity D can be defined as the distance between the two projections of the obstacle cast from O1 and O2 on the ground plane (the z=0 plane), i.e., the two points of coordinates $(x_{p1}, y_{p1}, 0)$ and $(x_{p2}, y_{p2}, 0)$. Moreover, it is interesting to represent the disparity D as composed by the two components D_x and D_y. For a binocular sensor with two conventional cameras, O1 and O2 are represented by the optical centres of the cameras and the stereo disparity is independent of the orientation of the cameras.

Setting the position of the two cameras, it is possible to compute D_x and D_y as functions of the coordinates of P:

$$D_x = h \cdot (|z_1 - z_2| / | z_1 z_2 |) \cdot | X - X_0 | = h \cdot K \cdot | X - X_0 |$$

$$D_y = h \cdot (|z_1 - z_2| / | z_1 z_2 |) \cdot | Y - Y_0 | = h \cdot K \cdot | Y - Y_0 |$$

where (x_1, y_1, z_1) and (x_2, y_2, z_2) represent the coordinates of O1 and O2, respectively, (X, Y, h) the coordinates of P, $X_0 = (x_2 z_1 - x_1 z_2)/(z_1 - z_2)$ and K is a constant. This result shows that there is a straight line (of equation $X = X_0$) along which any obstacle produces a null disparity independently of its height. A similar result can be obtained for D_y.

3.2.2. IPT-based obstacle detection

The idea of using inverse perspective for obstacle detection was first introduced in [17]. If one applies the inverse perspective transform (IPT) with respect to the same plane to a pair of stereo images, everything that lies on that plane looks the same in both views, while everything that does not is distorted differently, depending on the geometry of the two cameras through which the stereo pair is acquired. This property is particularly useful for tasks in which a relevant

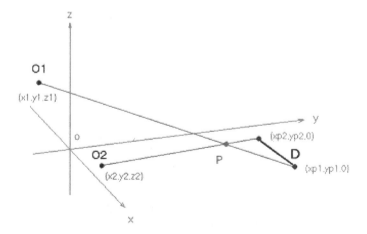

Figure 7. Schematic representation of the stereo disparity D obtained by looking at the point P from the two points of view O1 and O2. The x-y axis plane is the ground reference plane.

reference plane can be easily found. This is the case for navigation, either for vehicles travelling on roads (see [6,7,18] for a review on the subject) or for indoor-operating autonomous robots [10].

Three steps are therefore usually required to detect obstacles based on stereo vision:

- application of the IPT to each of the two images;
- subtraction of one image from the other one to compute differences;
- remapping of the regions where obstacle candidates can be found on at least one of the acquired images, to label pixels either as obstacle or free space.

3.3. *Omnidirectional Stereo Systems*

The same considerations made regarding stereo systems made up of conventional sensors can be extended to systems in which the two sensors are catadioptric omnidirectional sensors. The only difference is the fact that, instead of the optical centre of the cameras, in this case we will have to refer to the point on the mirrors which correspond to the reflection of the point of interest. As will be shown more formally in the following, in this case, the positions of the two reference points O1 and O2 depend on the coordinates of P. Figure 8 shows the simulation of a stereo omnidirectional systems and of two virtual images of a RoboCup environment. The two mirrors of the simulated system are co-axial. In this case, the property by which rotation-symmetric mirrors with a discontinuity in the vertex can reduce reflection of lower objects which cross the axis up to making it collapse into a single point, is essential for this kind of system to work properly. Therefore, this constraint will have to be added to the specifications, when designing such systems.

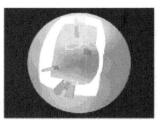

Figure 8. The simulation of a possible omnidirectional stereo systems with two views of a virtual RoboCup scene.

3.4. *Hybrid Omnidirectional/pin-hole Systems (HOPS)*

HOPS [3] (of which two prototypes are shown in Figure 9) is a hybrid vision sensor that integrates omnidirectional vision with traditional pin-hole vision, to overcome the limitations of the two approaches.

If a certain height is needed by the traditional camera to achieve a reasonable field of view, the top of the omnidirectional sensor may provide a base for the conventional sensor that can lean on it or be set aside it, as shown in Figure 9. In the prototype shown to the right, the conventional camera looks down with a tilt angle of about 60° with respect to the ground plane and has a field of view of about 80°. To obtain both horizontal and vertical disparity between the two images, it is positioned off the centre of the device. The 'blind sector' caused by the upper camera cable on the lower sensor is placed at an angle of 180° with respect to a conventional 'front view', in order to relegate it to the back of the device. If a lower point of view is acceptable for the traditional camera, the camera can also be placed below the omnidirectional sensor, provided it is out of the field of view of the latter, as in the prototype on the left. An example of the images that can be acquired through the two sensors of the first prototype to the left of Figure 9 is provided in Figure 10.

Figure 9. Two prototype HOPS systems.

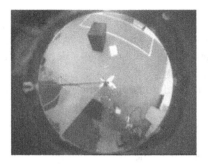 

Figure 10. Example of images that can be acquired through the omnidirectional sensor (left) and through the conventional camera (right) of HOPS.

The aims with which HOPS was designed are accuracy, efficiency and versatility. The joint use of a conventional camera and of an omnidirectional sensor provides HOPS with different and complementary features: while the conventional camera can be used to acquire detailed information about a limited region of interest, as happens in human foveal vision, the omnidirectional sensor provides wide-range, but less detailed, information about the surroundings of the system, as in human peripheral vision.

HOPS, therefore, suits several kinds of applications as, for example, self-localization or obstacle detection, and makes it possible to implement peripheral/foveal active vision strategies: the wide-range sensor is used to acquire a rough representation of a large area around the system and to localize the objects or areas of interest, while the conventional camera is used to enhance the resolution with which these areas are then analysed. The different features of the two sensors can be exploited in both a stand-alone fashion as well as in a combined use. In particular, HOPS can be used as a stereo sensor to extract three-dimensional information about the scene that is being observed.

3.4.1. Computing disparity in HOPS

With reference to Figure 7, in the case of HOPS, O1 is the optic center of the conventional camera, while O2 is the point on the mirror surface that reflects the image of point P onto the camera in the omnidirectional sensor. This means that it is possible to reason as in the case of two traditional cameras, with the only difference that now the position of one of the two reference points O1 and O2 depends on the coordinates of P. In this case we obtain that:

$$D_x = h \cdot (|z_1 - f(X,Y,h)| / |z_1 \cdot f(X,Y,h)|) \cdot |X - X_0(X,Y,h)|$$

$$D_y = h \cdot (|z_1 - f(X,Y,h)| / |z_1 \cdot f(X,Y,h)|) \cdot |Y - Y_0(X,Y,h)|$$

where $f(X,Y,h)$ is the z coordinate of O2, function of the position of P. The only difference with the result reported above is that there exists a different straight line of null disparity for every possible position of the obstacle. As just shown above, the position of this line depends only on the coordinates of O1 and O2. If the conventional camera had been placed on the plane (x=c) passing through the symmetry axis of the omni-directional sensor and parallel to the plane x=0, X_0 would equal c where X equals c, so that all the central part of the visible area would have null or very low stereo disparity. For this reason it is advisable that the conventional camera be placed as off this plane as possible, when stereo disparity is expected to provide useful information.

3.4.2. *3.4.2.* Obstacle detection using HOPS

The generalization of IPT to any kind of sensor, as discussed in a previous section, makes it possible to use HOPS as a stereo sensor for IPT-based obstacle detection, as previously described.

This opportunity was tested in our laboratory by installing one of HOPS prototypes on a mobile robot and using it as its only sensor for navigation. In the experiments we performed, the robot had to reach a goal moving on a floor on which a few objects were scattered. Some of these were just flat objects, like sheets of paper, which would not interfere with robot motion. Some other objects, instead, had significant height, and were to be avoided by the robot.

Figure 11. Test 1: (left) a large obstacle and an apparent obstacle separate the robot from the goal; (centre) the robot avoids the large one and ignores the apparent one; (right) and reaches the goal. Test 2: (left) the robot avoids the notebook bag; (centre) and the waste-paper basket, ignoring the sheet of paper; (right) and reaches the goal.

Two experiments were carried out. In the first one, the robot had just to circumvent a large obstacle, while, in the second one, the robot had to pass between two smaller objects. In both cases the robot was required to ignore all 'apparent obstacles'. In particular the robot was to ignore all flat objects lying on the floor. In fact, they appear and would be treated in the same way as actual obstacles if only two-dimensional information is taken into account, due to their color, which is different from the floor color. Figure 11 shows a few frames taken from the video of this experiment[b].

4. Final Remarks

In this chapter we have tried to offer a panoramic view, mainly based on examples of practical applications, of the different kinds of vision systems which can be used in mobile robotics.

We have mainly focused on less conventional systems, such as omnidirectional systems and multi-sensor systems, which offer stereo vision capabilities. Specific attention was devoted to a peculiar hybrid configuration, we have termed HOPS, in which a conventional camera is associated to an omnidirectional one. This configuration is aimed at developing applications in which the properties of both kinds of sensors are requested. Besides their use as complementary sensors, we have discussed the use of HOPS as a stereo sensor.

Although, because of its practical-example based nature and to our specific interests, the chapter is far from offering a complete and homogeneous review of the field, it provides a very general introduction to vision sensors for mobile robotics, while showing some original results obtained with unconventional ensembles of different kinds of sensors.

References

1. G. Adorni, S. Cagnoni, and M. Mordonini, *Proc. Asian Conf. on Computer Vision*, 601 (2000).
2. G. Adorni, L. Bolognini, S. Cagnoni, and M. Mordonini, *Proc. 7th AI*IA Conf.*, Springer LNAI 2175, 344 (2001).
3. G. Adorni, S. Cagnoni, M. Mordonini, and A. Sgorbissa, *Proc. OMNIVIS03*, IEEE (2003). (available only on CD-Rom or online at http://www.cs.wustl.edu/pless/omnivisFinal/cagnoni.pdf)
4. G. Adorni, S. Cagnoni, S. Enderle, G. Kraetschmar, M. Mordonini, M. Plagge, M. Ritter, S. Sablatnög, and A. Zell, *J. Robotics and Autonomous Systems*, **36 n. 2-3**, 103 (2001).

---

[b] The full video can be watched and downloaded at
http://www.ce.unipr.it/people/cagnoni/Filmati/caretta.mpg

5. S. Baker and S. K. Nayar, in R. Benosman and S. B. Kang (eds.), *Panoramic Vision: Sensors, Theory and Applications*, Springer-Verlag Monographs in Computer Science, 39 (2001).
6. M. Bertozzi, A. Broggi, and A. Fascioli, *Image and Vision Computing Journal*, **16 n.8**, 585 (1998).
7. S. Bohrer, T. Zielke, and V. Freiburg, *Proc. Intelligent Vehicles '95*, 276 (1995).
8. A. Bonarini, P. Aliverti, and M. Lucioni, *IEEE Trans. on Instrumentation and Measurement*, **49 n.3**, 509 (2000).
9. L. Delahoche, B. Maric, C. Pégard, and P. Vasseur, *Proc. IEEE/RSJ Int. Conf. on Intelligent Robots and Systems*, 718 (1997).
10. C. Drocourt, L. Delahoche, C. Pégard, and C. Cauchois, *Proc. IEEE/RSJ Int. Conf. on Intelligent Robots and Systems*, 960 (1999).
11. N. Guil, J. Villalba, and E.L. Zapata, *IEEE Trans. on Image Processing*, **4 n.11**, 1541 (1995).
12. J. S. Gutmann, T. Weigel, and B. Nebel, *Proc. 1999 IEEE/RSJ Int. Conf. on Intelligent Robots and Systems*, 1412 (1999).
13. R. A. Hicks and R. Bajcsy, *Proc. 2nd Workshop on Perception for Mobile Agents*, 82 (1999).
14. H. Ishiguro, in R. Benosman and S. B. Kang (eds.), *Panoramic Vision: Sensors, Theory and Applications*, Springer-Verlag Monographs in Computer Science, 23 (2001).
15. H. Ishiguro, K. Kato, and M. Barth, in R. Benosman, and S. B. Kang (eds.), *Panoramic Vision: Sensors, Theory and Applications*, Springer-Verlag Monographs in Computer Science, 377 (2001).
16. P. Lima, A. Bonarini, C. Machado, F. Marchese, F. Ribeiro, and D. Sorrenti, *J. of Robotics and Autonomous Systems*, **36 n. 3**, 87 (2001).
17. H. A. Mallot, H. H. Bülthoff, J. J. Little, and S. Bohrer, *Biolog. Cybern.*, **64**, 167 (2001).
18. K. Onoguchi, N. Takeda, and M. Watanabe, *IEICE Trans. Inf. & Syst.*, **E81-D n. 9**, 1006 (1998).
19. M. Plagge, R. Günther, J. Ihlenburg, D. Jung, and A. Zell, *RoboCup-99 Team Descriptions*, 200 (1999) (*available at* http://www.ep.liu.se/ea/cis/1999/006/cover.html).
20. T. Sogo, H. Ishiguro, and M. Trivedi, in R. Benosman and S. B. Kang (eds.), *Panoramic Vision: Sensors, Theory and Applications*, Springer-Verlag Monographs in Computer Science, 359 (2001).
21. Y. Yagi, S. Kawato, and S. Tsuji, *IEEE Trans. on Robotics and Automation*, **10 n.1**, 11 (1994).

A NOTE ON PICTORIAL INFORMATION

VITO DI GESÙ

Dipartimento di Matematica ed Applicazioni, Università di Palermo
Via Archirafi 34, 90123, Palermo

The chapter introduces new entropy measures that use the image information content such as grey levels and their topological distribution in the image domain in order to perform the classification of the image itself. The main aim of the chapter is to study the role of the image entropy in perceptual tasks and to compare the proposed approach with others well-known methods. Experiments have been carried out on medical images (mammograms) due to their variability and complexity. The image entropy approach seems to work quite well and it is less time-consuming if compared with the other methods.

1. Introduction

Visual science is considered one of the most important fields of investigation in perception as a matter of fact that a large part of the empirical knowledge we have about the world is based on the visual perception. In order to fully understand vision mechanisms we need to consider the interaction and the integration among all sensors of perception (e.g. hearing, touch, sense of smell). Moreover, the information that comes from our sensors to the brain is elaborated by using also mental models (mental information) that are stored somewhere. Furthermore, it has been always a challenging problem to understand how we see and how we interpret visual scene surrounding us. One question arises *What processes fill the gap between the picture-like information on the retina and conceptually structured perceptual representations*?

Visual perception is an interesting investigation topic because of its presence in most human activities. It can be used for communication, decoration and ritual purposes. Visual information depends on the context. Images may transfer emotion (see Figure 1). We could call this kind of information *emotional*.

Figure 1. Women Playing Music (Tintoretto 1518-1594, Venice).

Figure 2. Graffiti representing acrobats (Addaura caves, Palermo, Italy).

On the other hands, images may increase our knowledge; for example, the scene of hunting men represented by graffiti on walls prehistoric caves in Figure 2 tells us about the style of life of prehistoric men. We call this kind of pictorial information *knowledge acquisition*. Note that, graffiti can be considered the first example of visual language that uses an iconic technique to pass on history. They may also suggest us how prehistoric men internalized external world.

The intrinsic meaning of an image depends also on the expectation and the resulting perceived may influence our decision, this is the case of medical diagnostic (see Figure 3). In this case pictorial information allows us to *discover* a cue.

On the other hand, a static scene may transfer dynamic information telling us how the world will evolve. This is the case of the cartoon photogram in Figure 4 where the lion is approaching its cub. It is proud and loving, we could image the discussion even without the help of sound.

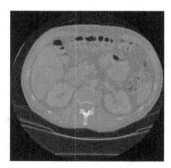

Figure 3. CTA image of a patient's abdomen.

Figure 4. Dynamic information from a single photogram.

Verbal messages can be added to pictorial data that involve the integration of different sources of information (see Figure 5).

All these examples do not exhaust the taxonomy related to pictorial information, but they highlight how complex is the definition of information when the semantic is included in the problem.

In this case, the computation of a system information by means of the entropy as defined by Shannon [1] could be unsatisfactory. In fact, emotional or linguistic features can not be assimilated to those used in thermodynamics, even if they still characterize changes in the system status.

Subjective experience may play a fundamental role whenever *inexactness* and *vagueness* can not be modeled by probabilistic reasoning; in fact, *cloudy* features may exist that are not describable in terms of probability distributions. For example, the *beauty of some thing* or the *tallness of a man.* In all these cases, education, fashion and global knowledge may play a crucial role in making decisions.

The problem of modelling non numerical information is of great interest in artificial systems. Soft computing and fuzzy sets can provide a powerful mathematical tool to model abstract concepts, allowing the definition of functions that satisfy entropic properties.

Figure 5. Linguistic and visual integration.

Fuzzy Set Theory was formalised by Zadeh at the University of California in 1965 [2]. What Zadeh proposed is very much a paradigm shift that first gained acceptance in the Far East and its successful application has ensured its adoption around the world. Crisp concept of *true* and *false* are replaced by continuous degree of true ranging in the interval [0,1]. Quoting Zadeh:

> ... *For a long time humankind has endeavoured to understand the laws of the surrounding world and has made continuous attempts to describe the phenomena occurring in the world. Naturally we want to achieve the most adequate descriptions by means of exact and precise terms. Mathematical language should be the best tool to express such descriptions; however, the language of set theory and extensional logic is sometimes insufficient...*

The framework of fuzzy sets allowed us to define entropy based functions that have been used in image and signal analysis to perform deconvolution [3] and segmentation [4], to measure the pictorial information [5], and to define image differences [6,7,8]. Entropic measure has been used for medical diagnosis in [9,10].

2. Processing Pictorial Information

Pictorial information processing (*PIP*) is developed throughout several layers of increasing abstraction that corresponds to a set of iterated transformations.

One of the main tasks of a *PIP* is the ability to focus the computation in areas of interest, based on the maximization of an expected utility criterion that includes costs and benefits. This feature is also named *visual attention* or *selective vision*. Visual attention is also included in natural vision system, and it allows to reduce the computation time, avoiding redundant computation [11].

Moreover, *PIP* should be able to adapt its *behavior* depending on the current goal and the nature of the input data. Such flexibility can be obtained in systems able to interact dynamically with the environment. The term *active vision* has been coined, to address such kind of visual computation [12].

In the active vision paradigm, the basic components of the visual system are visual behaviors tightly integrated with the actions they support. Because the cost of generating and updating a complete, detailed model of the environment is too high, the development of this approach to vision is vital for achieving robust, real-time perception of the real world.

The search of regions of interest is usually followed by a matching procedure that performs objects *classification* or the *clustering* of *relevant features*. There are a number of feature dimensions (e.g., position, colour, size, orientation, gradient, form, trajectory, etc.) that govern the grouping of elements of the receptive field into objects by the following Gestalt rules: *neighbouring elements with similar features tend to belong to one and the same object; proximity and similarity are the main factors in perception* [13].

It follows that the extraction of information depending on grouping rules may be defined on the basis of the problem we are considering. In the case of visual information graphs can be associated to each level of the recognition process.

Moreover, visual pattern recognition is a process that is performed throughout several layers of increasing abstraction, corresponding to a set of iterated transformations. Therefore, models of visual processes are developed through a hierarchy of graphs each corresponding to a different feature space.

For example, Di Gesù and Zahn in [14] developed a new method to recognize lines based on hierarchy of different space starting from a set of points in two-dimensional space. Here, curves are considered as ordered sequences of lines or edges as primitive elements of a recognition system. The algorithm firstly detects short sequences of closely spaced points by using single link algorithm based on the Minimum Spanning Tree. The result is a set of very oblong (nearly linear) shapes, named segments. Then, segments are linked together into longer curves with slowly varying directionality. The clustering of segments is performed by a *KNN* link algorithm that uses a measure of closeness or similarity between segments based on their reciprocal orientation and spatial position. This kind of procedure can be extended by considering hierarchies of space of increasing complexity (see Figure 6).

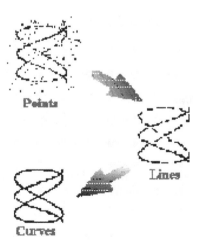

Figure 6. Hierarchical computation from points to curves.

2.1. *Soft Vision*

Fuzzy sets provide methods for the analysis of images [15]. Their application cover most of the analysis, from low to high level vision.

For example, *fuzzy-convolvers* have been designed whose kernel values depends on both the point spread function of the detector and the local pixel-relations. Extension of mathematical morphology to grey levels images has been carried out by using fuzzy-sets in [16]. This extension is based on the interpretation of the gray level of a given pixel as its belonging degree to **X**, and by using *min/max* operators.

High level vision process could be considered as a *complex pattern matching* in the sense that recognition is the evaluation of a fitting algorithm applied to heterogeneous information (visual and textual). This fitting is realized throughout the visit of pictorial data-base and knowledge-base. Moreover recognition systems must be able to handle uncertainty, and to include subjective interpretation. For example, an *intelligent system* should be able to *evaluate and understand* the following fuzzy-propositions:

a) *the chair, beyond the table, is small;*

b) *the chair, beyond the table, is very small;*

c) *the chair, beyond the table, is quite small;*

d) *few objects have straight medial axis.*

Where *small* is a fuzzy verbal predicate, *very* and *quite* are fuzzy attributes. The evaluation depends on the *meaning* that is given to small, very and quite. Moreover the objects chair and table, and the relation *beyond* must be recognized with some degree of truth. The proposition d) contains the fuzzy quantifier *few*.

3. Applications

3.1. *Image Segmentation*

The main problem in image analysis is to extract the signal from the background and the selection of the important compounds. This phase is also said *image segmentation*. The success of this phase may influence all recognition process. The dog in Figure 7 shows how the segmentation process is complex and not easy to implement in artificial systems.

Figure 7. The hidden dog.

Pre-attentive processes may help in performing image segmentation. For example the applications of local symmetry operators may help to extract proper segments from very complex images. The reason is that attentive processes are able to focus the attention on the *relevant* regions of the scene reducing the redundancy of the image data. For example, in Figure 8a the operator *DST* (Digital Symmetry Transform) [17] is applied to the image in Figure 1. Figure 8b shows the regions of interest that have been highlighted by the *DST*.

It is interesting to note that the entropy of the input image, X, of dimensions $N{\times}M$ is usually greater than the entropy of the pre-processed $DST(X)$, where the entropy used is the classical one, with the gray levels, p_{ij}, interpreted as a measure of probability of the pixel (i,j):

$$H(X) = -\sum_{i=1}^{N}\sum_{j=1}^{M} p_{ij} \log p_{ij} \qquad (i,j) \in X$$

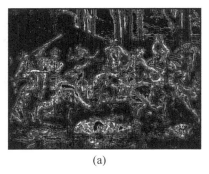

(a)

(b)

Figure 8. Pre-attentive process: (a) *DST* of the painting in Figure 1; (b) selected regions of interest.

In our example $H(X)$=5.24 and $H(DST(X))$=2.53, note that the entropy of the image, S, containing the selected regions is $H(S\ (X))$=2.63. This means that redundancy has been reduced maintaining a good image quality in the interesting parts.

3.2. *Texture Analysis*

In the previous example the entropy is computed in the whole image. In some cases entropy functions can be computed locally in sub-images, A, of X. This kind of computation allow us to detect local structure of the image and the application of the local entropy operator is able to detect non regular textures. For example, in Figures 9(a,b) are shown the input image, X, and its DST. Figures 9(c,d) show the effect of cutting the gray levels less than a threshold $\varphi>0$.

Regular textures can be detected using a measure of entropy that is function of a given correlation step τ (in pixels). We call this information measure *correlated entropy*.

$$H(X) = \sum_{x \in X} f(x) \otimes f(y) \qquad \begin{aligned} x &\equiv \left(g_x, i_x, j_x\right) \\ y &\equiv \left(g_y, i_x + \tau, j_x + \tau\right) \end{aligned}$$

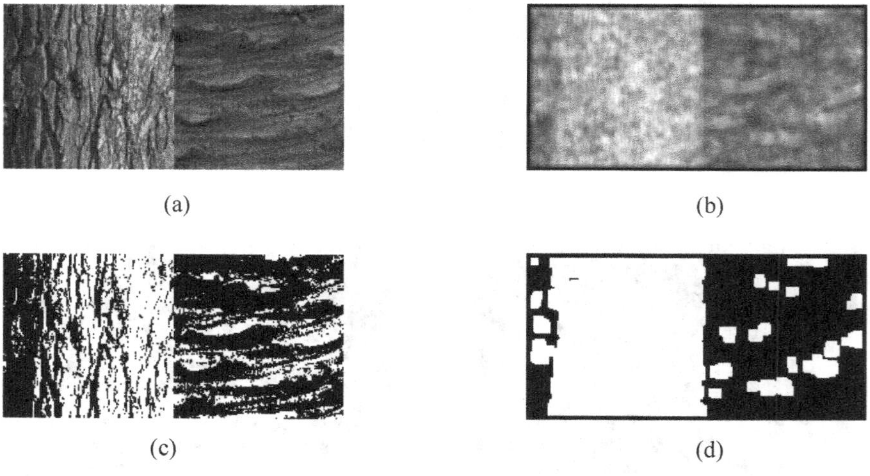

(a)   (b)

(c)   (d)

Figure 9. (a) X; (b) $DST(X)$; (c) threshold of X with $\varphi>0$; (d) threshold of $DST(X)$ with $\varphi>0$.

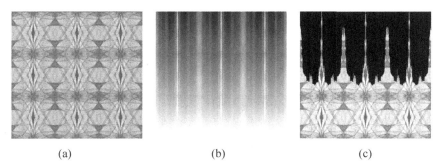

(a)   (b)   (c)

Figure 10. (a) *X*; (b) *DST(X)*; (c) regular texture in the direction of the horizontal axes.

Figure 10(a,b,c) shows an example of detection of regular texture.

3.3. *Object Matching*

Visual tasks are often based on the evaluation of distances or similarities between objects represented in an appropriate feature space. For example, an image querying system, grounded on the image content, processes the query on the basis of a matching procedure, that assigns the unknown to the closest prototype. For example, in [18] a new method is proposed for similarity-based partial image retrieval that greatly reduces the required storage space for indexes.

In the last years, several definitions of distance between images have been considered [19,20]. The choice of the feature space (type and number of the parameters describing the image) is one of the crucial aspect of the problem. *Global* features, directly derived from the gray levels (e.g. first and second order statistics, color), can be used to define measures of similarity. However, global features may produce wrong results; for example, quite different images may have the same histogram. *Structural* features (e.g. skeleton, medial axis, convex hull, symmetry) are very sensitive to the shape of the objects in the scene.

In this case matching algorithms may be necessary to test the correspondence between relational graphs and the cost of computation may grow exponentially. Distance functions, based on the combination of global and contextual information, seem to be more adequate to characterize differences between images.

In many cases both probabilistic reasoning and standard geometry may be faulty and *fuzzy* approaches can be more promising. Fuzzy distances, based on entropic functions may provide a better performance in image matching problems [6,7]. For example, the following entropic similarities have been tested on the pictorial database JACOB [21,22]:

$$G_0(\delta)=-\frac{\delta(x,y)}{2}\log\frac{\delta(x,y)}{2}-\frac{1-\delta(x,y)}{2}\log\frac{1-\delta(x,y)}{2}$$

$$G_1(\delta)=\delta(x,y)e^{1-\delta(x,y)}$$

$$G_2(\delta)=2\delta(x,y)\left(1-\frac{\delta(x,y)}{2}\right)$$

$$G_3(\delta)=\sqrt{\delta(x,y)}$$

where, the variable δ is a normalized distance function. Entropic similarities, G_i ($i=0,1,2,3$), range in the interval $[0,1]$ and their trend in function of δ is given in Figure 11.

These distances have been named entropic for two reasons: a) their analytical form derives from entropy functions; b) they adapt classical distance functions to the feature space as a matter of fact that they model the distance function δ expanding it where it is smaller (close to the origin) and performing a contraction where it is larger (close to 1).

Table 1 shows a comparison of the entropic similarity G_0 with three standard ones that are used in the literature. The results obtained with G_1, G_2, and G_3 are not reported because comparable with those obtained with G_0, where D is the Euclidean distance, AD is the averaged distance, CO is the correlation distance. Their mathematical definitions can be found in [23].

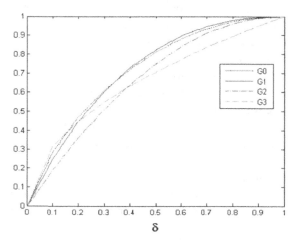

Figure 11. Trend of the entropic similarities with δ.

Table 1. Comparison of G_0 with classical measure of similarities.

Similarity	Correct matches	Mismatches
G_0	92.6	7.4
D	81.5	18.5
CO	80.0	20.0
AD	75.5	24.5

4. Discussion and Final Remarks

The chapter analyzes the concept of visual information from several perspectives. Information is associated to changes in the status of a system. The definition of the information content of a system in terms of its entropy computed in the phase space is not always satisfying. For example, emotional, and linguistic information can't be computed via entropy functions. In these cases fuzzy-sets could be a useful tool to represents abstract thinking in a computer. On the other hand, the definition of entropic functions based on the properties of convex and not decreasing functions are appropriate for handling numerical properties of an image. The problem of analyzing pictorial information in this cases can be formulated as the alternation of attentive processes and matching algorithms. For example, several low-level visual tasks can be handled using measures of local information. Entropic distances are useful in image matching problems; they show an interesting property of expansion/compression, that can be usefully used to group in finer classes elements close to the origin and to group in broadest classes elements close to the frontiers of the distance space.

References

1. C. E. Shannon, "A mathematical theory of communication," *Bell System Technical Journal,* **27**, pp. 379-423 and 623-656, July and October, (1948).
2. L. A. Zadeh, *"Fuzzy sets"*, *Inform. Control*, **8**, pp.338-353, (1965).
3. F. Kossentini, M.J.T. Smith, C.F. Barnes, "Image coding using entropy-constrained residual vector quantization", *in IEEE Transactions on Image Processing* , **4** , pp.1349-1357, (1995).
4. Z. Xiong, K. Ramchandran, and M. T. Orchard, "Space-frequency quantization for wavelet image coding", in *IEEE Transactions on Image Processing*, **6**, N.5, pp. 677-693, (1997).
5. J. Skilling, R.K. Bryan, "Maximum entropy image reconstruction: general algorithm", *Month. Notices Roy. Astronom. Soc*, **211**, pp. 111-124, (1984).
6. V. Di Gesù, S. Roy, "Pictorial indexes and soft image distances", in *Lecture Notes in Computer Science*, N.R. Pal and M. Sugeno (Eds.), pp. 200-215 (2002).

7. V. Di Gesù, S. Roy, "Fuzzy measures for image distance", *in proc of Advances in Fuzzy Systems and Intelligent Technologies*, F. Masulli, R. Parenti, G. Pasi (Eds.), Shaker Publishing, pp.156 -164, (2000).

8. J. Zachar, S.S. Iyengar, "Informaton theoretic similarity measures for content based image retrieval", *Journal of the American Society for Information Science and Technology*, **52**, N.10, pp. 856-857, (2001).

9. A. Casanova, V. Savona and S. Vitulano, "Entropy As A Feature In The Analysis And Classification Of Signals", *MDIC*, (2004).

10. A. Casanova, V. Di Gesù, G. Lo Bosco, S. Vitulano, "Entropy measures in Image Classification", *Human and Machine Perception 4: Communication, Interaction, and Integration*, V. Cantoni *et al.* (Eds.), World Scientific, Singapore, (2005).

11. C.M. Brown: Issue in selective perception. In Proc.11th IAPR Int. Conf. on Patt. Recog., *IEEE Computer Society Press*, Vol. A, pp.21-30, (1992).

12. Promising direction in active vision. Tech. Report CS 91-27, M.J. Swain and M. Stricker (Eds.), University of Chicago, (1991).

13. M. Wertheimer, "Untersuchungen zur Lehre von der Gestalt I. Prinzipielle Bemerkungen ", *Psychologische Forschung*, **1**, pp. 47-58, (1922).

14. V. Di Gesù, C.T. Zahn, "A general method to recognize two-dimensional dotted curves", in *Radiol. Clin.No.Amer, S.L.A.C Tech.Rep. 75/01*, Stanford University, (1975).

15. S.K. Pal and D.K.D. Majumder, "Fuzzy mathematical approach to pattern recognition", Jon Wiley & Sons, (1986).

16. V. Di Gesù, "Artificial Vision and Soft Computing", in *Fundamenta Informaticae,* **(37)**, pp.101-119, (1999).

17. V. Di Gesù, C. Valenti, "Symmetry operators in computer vision", in *Vistas in Astronomy*, Pergamon, **40**(4), pp. 461-468, (1996).

18. B. He, I. Ounis, "Inferring Query Performance Using Pre-retrieval Predictors", in *11th Symposium on String Processing and Information Retrieval (SPIRE 2004)*, October 5-8, Padova, Italy, (2004).

19. A. Del Bimbo, E. Vicario, S. Berretti, "Spatial arrangement of color in retrieval by visual similarity", in *Pattern Recognition*, **35**(8), pp. 1661-1674 (2002).

20. P.M. Kelly, T.M. Cannon, and D.R. Hush, "Query by image example: the CANDID approach", in *Proc. of the SPIE: Storage and Retrieval for Image and Video Databases III*, **2420**, pp. 238-248, (1995).

21. E. Ardizzone, V. Di Gesù, M. La Cascia, C. Valenti, "Content Based Indexing of Image and Video Databases", in *Proc.12th ICPR, IEEE*, (1996).

22. M. La Cascia, E. Ardizzone, "JACOB: Just a content-based query system for video databases", *Proc. of ICASSP '96*, Atlanta, (1996).

23. V. Di Gesù, V. Starovoitov, "Distance-based functions for image comparison", in *Pattern Recognition Letters,* **20**, pp. 207-214, (1999).

BIOMEDICAL SIGNAL PROCESSING AND MODELING: MULTISCALE AND MULTIORGAN INTEGRATION OF INFORMATION

SERGIO CERUTTI [†]

Department of Bioengineering Polytechnic University, Piazza Leonardo da Vinci 32, 20133 Milano, Italy

Biomedical signals carry important information about the behavior of the living systems under studying. A proper processing of these signals allows in many instances to obtain useful physiological and clinical information. Many advanced algorithms of signal and image processing have recently been introduced in such an advanced area of research and therefore important selective information is obtainable even in presence of strong sources of noise or low signal/noise ratio. Traditional stationary signal analysis together with innovative methods of investigation of dynamical properties of biological systems and signals in second-order or in higher-order approaches (i.e., in time-frequency, time-variant and time-scale analysis, as well as in non linear dynamics analysis) provide a wide variety of even complex processing tools for information enhancement procedures. Another important innovative aspect is also remarked: the integration between signal processing and modeling of the relevant biological systems is capable to directly attribute patho-physiological meaning to the parameters obtained from the processing and viceversa the modeling fitting could certainly be improved by taking into account the results from signal processing procedure. Such an integration process could comprehend parameters and observations detected at different scales, at different organs and with different modalities. This approach is reputed promising for obtaining an olistic view of the patient rather than an atomistic one which considers the whole as a simple sum of the single component parts.

1. Introduction

The processing of biomedical signals is an important step towards the obtaining of objective data from the analysis of living systems. The aims could be: i) to improve the physiological knowledge of the system; ii) to provide quantitative data for clinical purposes (diagnosis, therapy and rehabilitation) [7][17][24] [25]. A wide variety of processing algorithms are traditionally applied to biomedical signals. Due to the fact that such signals are often quite difficult to be processed and characterized by low signal/noise ratio, practically all the methods introduced in the signal processing arena have been more or less applied in the different approaches of biomedical signal processing: stationary and non stationary signal analysis, second-order or higher order approaches,

---

[†] Work partially supported by a EU Grant, *My-Heart Project*, 2004.

with deterministic or stochastic methods, in time domain and in frequency domain, using linear and non linear algorithms, etc.

New paradigms related to a new concept of biomedical signal processing are considered important. In the following, an approach is described which considers signal processing together with modeling of the relevant biological systems under studying, as well as an integration of the real information which is obtained at different scales, using different investigation modalities, with different organs. An integrated view of all this obtained information, generally realized through a multidisciplinary pathway which involves various and different competences and professionals, might produce a precious enhancement of information, thus providing a better knowledge of the underlying systems.

2. Signal Processing and Modeling of Biological Systems

A basic issue of innovative biomedical signal processing procedures is that a stronger link is required between modeling of biological systems and processing of the signals involved [3][5][9]. Most often, in fact, researchers who do modeling do not do signal processing. A well-trained biomedical engineer is capable to integrate the knowledge which is required to deal with models and with signal processing procedures and algorithms. A major innovative tool would be the improvement of medical knowledge through a cooperative process between signal processing and modeling, along the way indicated in Figure 1.

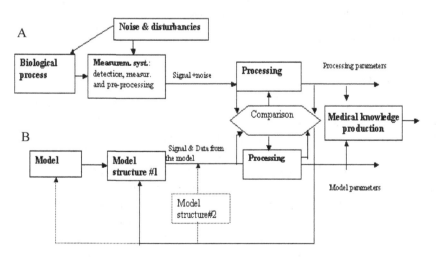

Figure 1. Integration between biomedical signal processing (channel A) and biological modeling (channel B) to create medical knowledge.

We may define one channel A to produce information (upper part of the figure) which is connected to the processing of biological signals and one channel B (lower part of the figure) which is connected to the modeling of the relevant biological system. The "processing" block takes information from the signals derived from the biological process under studying, as well as from the modeling of the physiological system. As an example, we may consider cardiovascular system (and in particular the physiological mechanisms which make the heart rate to change on a beat-to-beat basis). The signals involved may be heart rate variability (HRV) and/or arterial blood pressure variability (ABPV), while we have many physiological models in literature which describe the HRV and/or ABPV. Obviously, the signals have to be properly chosen and processed as well as the models suitably validated: at the end of the procedure a joint analysis of signal processing and modeling may indeed produce new information and knowledge, as depicted from the block in the right part of the figure.

Another example of this important integration of processing and modeling is given by the next figures (Fig. 2, 3 and 4). Figure 2 shows a well known model by Koepchen (1986) [13] in which many complex physiological relationships are schematically introduced for the description of the control of autonomic nervous system on cardiovascular functions: this is considered a typical (complex) model which is designed by taking into consideration only physiological observations. Figure 3 shows instead how in [2] we attempted to identify where various rhythms which are present on cardiovascular signals could be generated at central, autonomic and vascular levels. LF (low frequency) and HF (high frequency) are two basic rhythms which are found on cardiovascular variability signals (variability in heart rate: HRV and variability in arterial blood pressure: ABPV) [23]. Further, three signals were selected as information carriers of the complex physiological mechanisms underneath: heart period variability (RR series from the ECG signal), systolic blood pressure variability (series of systolic values from arterial blood pressure signal) and respiration. The model by Koepchen and the evidenced biosignals made us to design a black-box model, indicated in Figure 4, which describes the interactions between HRV (signal t), ABPV (signal s) and respiration (signal r) in the autonomic control of cardiovascular function. Of course, the model takes into account only a small part of the information which is suggested by the physiological model where we started from; in any case, after a validation of the black model as done in [3], it is possible to provide important physiological meaning to the blocks reported in Figure 4 (estimation of respiratory sinus arrhythmia, calculation of baroceptive gain in a closed-loop way, measurement of mechanical effect of heart rate on arterial blood pressure, gain and phase of the feedback regulating mechanisms, etc).

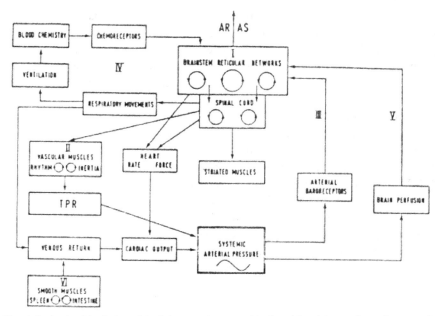

Figure 2. A physiological model of the complex central and peripheral interactions of autonomic regulations. From [13].

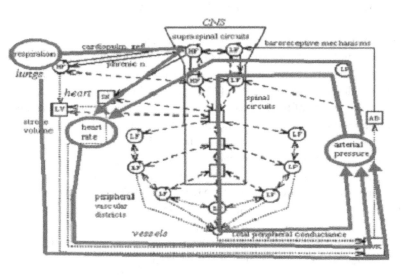

Figure 3. A model inspired to the structure of the physiological model reported in Figure 2. Here the signals from which to detect the information on autonomic regulations are evidenced (respiration, heart rate and arterial blood pressure). From [2].

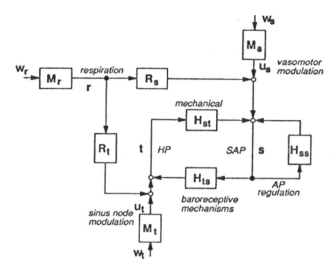

Figure 4. Block diagram of the black-box model describing the interactions between heart rate, arterial blood pressure and respiration in a double feedback loop, starting from the physiological considerations contained in Figs 2 and 3. From [3].

Another interesting approach of joint analysis of signal and model parameters is shown in Figure 5. Fig. 5a indicates a model originally developed by Kitney RI (1979) [12] and successively modified by Signorini (1997) [22], where there is a very simple description of the closed-loop regulation of blood pressure (signal y) according to different values of respiration signal (r). For simplicity r is assumed as a pure sinusoid indicated as equal to $\varepsilon \sin(2\pi ft)$. There is a negative feedback loop which induces oscillation in y signal due to the fact that there is also a non linear block in the forward path. According to the different values of the closed loop gain and the frequency of the respiration signal (by simplicity assumed as a pure sinusoid) we may have either a synchronization between respiration rate and blood pressure rate (i.e. they take the same frequency) or more complex behavior due to the non linear dynamics. In Fig. 5b there is the diagram of gain H1 as a function of f (frequency of respiratory signals). It is possible to see that a very complex phenomenon is evidenced: there is an area of 1:1 locking (synchronization between respiration and blood pressure) in the lower part of the figure, but also various transitions (bifurcations), when increasing H1, from synchronization to other forms of locking (i.e. 1:3), or to torus, or to torus breakdown with also a chaotic behavior just in the normal frequency range of respiration (0.20-0.30 Hz). Processing of arterial blood pressure signals confirm that, in this range, arterial blood pressure may present a chaotic behavior. This paradigmatic statement of "chaotic" behavior in the autonomic control of cardiovascular functions supports in many instances the hypothesis that the high complexity in the physiology of this system may be explained by a non linear dynamics. A non linear approach may thus be employed to better describe the model and hence a proper quantification of its behavior could be done through parameters of measurement of the strange attractor properties like Lyapunov exponents, Poincaré plots, fractal dimension and so on [10][21]. Disclosure from chaotic behavior or decreasing of their characteristic parameters are generally correlated to pathological conditions [14][26][15].

This is certainly another significant example of how integration between models and signal processing are able to produced new important physiological information.

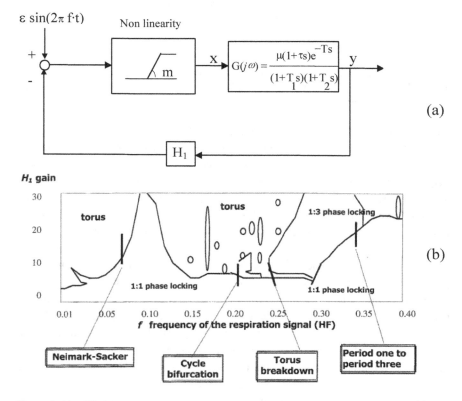

Figure 5. Simplified model of arterial blood pressure regulation (a), from [12] and modified by Signorini et al. [22]. Diagram of H_1 gain on the previous model as a function of the frequency f of respiration signal (b): a wide variety of complex behavior is noticed due to the non linear characteristics of the model, depending upon the value of f: phenomena of entrainment, bifurcation, synchronization and chaos are evidenced. For details, see text.

3. Multiorgan and Multiscale Integration

Another important issue which is connected to biomedical signal processing and the modeling of the relevant biological systems involved, consists in the integration of different information sources which may indeed constitute a unique data base relative to that single patient. That information integration is able to put together data which derive: 1) from different biological system or organs (multiorgan), i.e. integrating cardiovascular with respiratory and with endocryno-metabolic systems; 2) from different signal modalities (multimodality), i.e. making a "registration" of 3-D MRI cerebral data with 3-D EEG mapping, thus combining the high spatial resolution of the first technique with the high temporal resolution of the second one; 3) from different scale of information (multiscale), i.e. various pathologies may be better investigated by considering information at the various scales on which the phenomenon may be studied.

Some examples of this important integration paradigm will be illustrated below: here it is fundamental to state that in many instances there is also the need of integrating different professional figures, cultural backgrounds, training processes, personal attitudes and so on. Therefore is not simply a rather "technical" data integration which may allow the fulfillment of significant innovative results, but a more complex process of integration of knowledge from various and synergetic perspectives. From one side, encouraging a cooperative research among physiologists, clinicians, biologists, bioengineers, biophysicists, biomathematicians, etc, but also among experts of signal processing with colleagues experts in medical images, in molecular biology, in modeling at the various possible scales: from DNA/RNA scale, to gene/protein, to cell and cell fibers, to organ, to multiorgan analysis, to the single patient intended as a whole and unique system.

3.1. *Multiorgan Integration*

As an example of multiorgan integration, it is possible to cite the case of sleep studies. There, biological signal recordings, generally carried out during polysomnographic procedures, put into emphasis the fact that there is an involvement of several organs or systems.

Figure 6 shows a case of a patient who manifests the so-called restless-leg syndrome (RLLS), i.e. he undergoes a period of sleep (in stage 2) in which he presents a movement of legs, almost periodically. What is more interesting is that during this period there is a remarkable synchronization among biological rhythms of different origin: passing top-down in the figure, the first panel shows EEG tracing, where there are well visible phenomena of arousals, with a strong synchronization with the bursts of EMG signal (second panel) recorded at the level of tibial muscle (these bursts are obviously primarily associated with the RLLS). Further, the third panel shows the RR series (the beat-to-beat heart cycle) as detected from a standard ECG lead and the last panel shows the respiration signal, recorded via plethysmographic technique. Horizontal axis is the number of consecutive heart beats and all the four signals are aligned along this temporal occurrence. In order to obtain this common horizontal axis reference, the values of EEG and EMG in Fig. 6 are obtained as the mean values of instantaneous EEG and EMG taken between two consecutive cardiac cycle (RR's), while R is the respirogram, i.e. the value of respiration in correspondence with the R peak occurrence in ECG signal.

A very important synchronization among the four signals is noticed which is almost intriguing in its physiological interpretation: EMG bursts seem strictly correlated with acceleration/decelerations in heart rate and also with a kind of modulation mechanism in respiration which is even related to arousal phenomena in central nervous system (EEG signal). Important possible causal relationships among the signals coming from different physiological compartments (central and autonomic nervous systems, cardiorespiratory system and muscular system) are worth to be deeply and in more detail investigated [4].

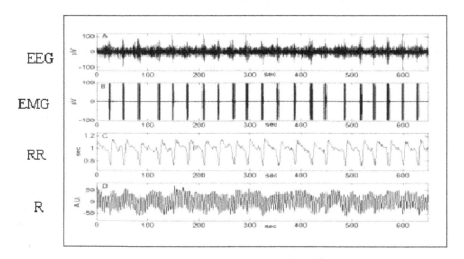

Figure 6. A case of a patient suffering from Restless-Leg Syndrome (RLLS). Signals are recorded during sleep (stage 2). From top to down: (i) scalp EEG lead which shows microarousals typical of CAP sleep microstructure; (ii) EMG activity recorded at the level of tibial muscle; (iii) heart rate variability signal plotted as the successive series of RR intervals detected on ECG lead; (iv) respiration signal (respirogram) detected in correspondence of each R occurrence on ECG lead. From [4].

3.2. *Multimodal Integration*

Another interesting information can be obtained through the fusion of signals and images detected from the same subject and from the same physiological system.

As an example, Figure 7 shows the fusion of data obtained via registration of MRI 3-D images with EEG 3-D mapping through scalp 10-20 EEG leads (from [6]). EEG electrical potential distribution can be in this way directly related to anatomical structure of the brain, as singled out from MRI technique. Properties of the two modalities are in some sense complementary (better spatial resolution in MRI images and better time resolution in EEG mapping) and the fusion of the two information do provide neurophysiologist and neurologist solid arguments for a better comprehension of the physiology underneath, as well as for a more accurate diagnosis for the planning of possible surgical intervention [18][19].

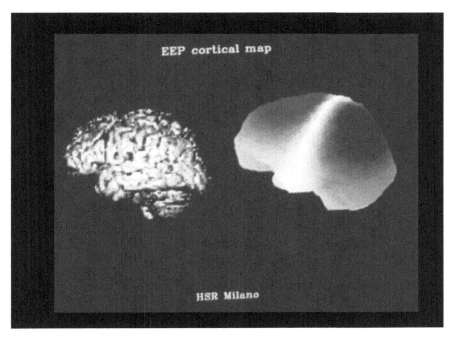

Figure 7. Example of fusion of 3-D MRI images (left) and EEG mapping (right). The EEG mapping is "registered" to MRI real data. From [6].

3.3. *Multiscale Integration*

Finally, it is worth mentioning another important integration which can be obtained along different observation scales. Traditionally, biological signal analysis is carried out at the level of organ or system to be investigated (i.e., ECG or EEG signal, arterial blood pressure, respiration and so on). It is very clear the advantage of correlating this information with that one obtained about the same system, but at different scale level, i.e. at cellular level or even at subcellular level (for example, analyzing possible genetic correlates or typical patterns of proteins or even DNA/RNA sequences). Biomedical engineering as a dedicated discipline may strongly contribute to this multiscale information processing [1].

A great effort is on course nowadays for creating very large databases for integrating such information (Physiome project to be connected with Genome and Proteome projects). In [8][11][20] a description of such a novel approach is given.

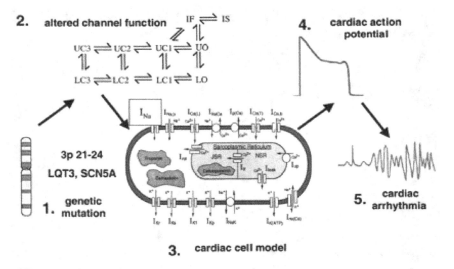

Figure 8. An example of integration of the information obtained at different scales of signal observations relative to "long QT3 syndrome": a mutation in SCN5A gene (1) produces an altered function in Na+ channels (2). A cardiac cell model explains the effect of this alteration (3), thus inducing a prolonged action potential in ventricular cells (4): this effect may cause dangerous tachyarrhythmias. From [20].

Figure 8 (from [20]) illustrates how an important cardiac pathology, the long-QT syndrome, can be efficiently studied at different scale level: a mutation in a portion of gene SCN5A which presents a phenotype compatible to long-QT3 type, is known to produce an altered function of Na+ channels. Through a proper model which describes the functioning of ventricular cells is possible to evidence that this alteration may induce a prolongation of QT duration, as detected on ECG tracing. This event is further correlated with an increased risk of ventricular tachyarrhythmias. Hence, the path is completed: from the genetic expression up to the disease manifestation [8][16]. Many different signal processing and modeling are involved in this paradigmatic example: an integration along the various scales of observation may undoubtedly contribute to a better understanding of the complex pathophysiological correlates.

4. Conclusion

As a conclusion, it is fundamental to stress an innovative role of biomedical signal processing. Not only new advanced algorithms have appeared on the research arena in the last years (here it is sufficient to mention only the time-variant or time-scale or time-frequency transformations and the various approaches in the area on non linear dynamics (fractal or chaotic systems)), which have determined new approaches to the problem of information enhancement from physiological system, but also a new integrative vision of biological phenomenon under studying plays a relevant role for obtaining new, important results in this fascinating topic.

Integration is certainly the keyword: actually, scientists have all the instruments to be able to put together information coming from different scales, different organs, different modalities, in a multivariate way. The modeling studying, typical of the Biomedical Engineering or Medical Physics worlds may help in the evaluation of parameters obtained from the signal/image processing and their validation from a physiological perspective. It is worth mentioning that such an advanced conception could bring a more olistic vision of the medical care rather than an atomistic one, thus contributing to treat the patient as a unicum (from genes to organs), and not as a sum of his/her parts.

References

1. M. Akay, Special Issue on Bioinformatics – Part I: Advances and Challenges, Part II: Genomics and Proteomics, *IEEE Proceedings*, vol.90, n.11 e 12 (2002).
2. G. Baselli, E. Caiani, A. Porta, N. Montano, M.G. Signorini and S. Cerutti, Biomedical signal processing and modeling in cardiovascular systems, *Crit Rev Biomed Eng.*, vol.30(1-3):55-84 (2002).
3. G. Baselli, S. Cerutti, S. Civardi, A. Malliani and M. Pagani, Cardiovascular variability signals: towards the identification of a closed-loop model of the neural control mechanisms, *IEEE Trans Biomed Eng.*, vol.35(12):1033-46(1988).

4. A.M. Bianchi, L. Riva, L. Ferini-Strambi, M. Zucconi and S. Cerutti, Synchronization of central and peripheral nervous system related to sleep microstructure, *Proceed. 2nd European MBE Conference*, pp. 486-487, Vienna (2002).

5. E.N. Bruce, *Biomedical Signal Processing and Signal Modelling*, J. Wiley (2001).

6. S. Cerutti and A.M. Bianchi, Metodi e tecniche innovative di elaborazione di segnali e immagini biomediche: nuovi strumenti per migliorare le conoscenze in fisiologia e in medicina, *Alta Frequenza*, vol.13, n.1:45-51(2001).

7. S. Cerutti, *Filtri Numerici per l'Elaborazione di Segnali Biologici*, CLUP ed, Milano (1983).

8. C.E. Clancy and Y. Rudy, Linking a genetic defect to its cellular phenotype in a cardiac arrhythmia, *Nature*, vol. 400(6744):566-569 (1999).

9. A. Cohen, *Biomedical Signal Analysis*, Vol. I, II, CRC Press (1986).

10. L. Glass and L.C. Mackey, *From Clocks to Chaos: The Rhythms of Life*, Princeton University Press (1988).

11. P. Hunter, P. Robbins and D. Noble, The IUPS human physiome project, *Pflugers Arch-Eur. J. Physiol.*, vol. 445:1-9 (2002).

12. R.I. Kitney, A nonlinear model for studing oscillations in the blood pressure control system, *J. Biomed. Eng.*, vol I,n. 2: 88-89 (1979).

13. H.P. Koepchen, History of studies and concepts of blood pressure wave, in: *Mechanisms of blood pressure waves* (Miyakawa K., Koepchen, H.P., Polosa C. eds): 3-23, Springer-Verlag (1984).

14. M.C. Mackey and J.C. Milton, Dynamical diseases, *Ann N Y Acad.Sc.*, vol.504:16-32 (1987).

15. C.-K. Peng, S. Havlin, J.M. Hausdorff, J.E. Mietus, H.E. Stanley and A.L. Goldberger, Fractal mechanisms and heart rate dynamics long-range correlation and their breakdown with diseases, *Journal of Electrocardiology*, vol.28: 59-65 (1995).

16. S.G. Priori, P.J. Schwartz, C. Napolitano, R. Bloise, E. Ronchetti, M. Grillo, A. Vicentini, C. Spazzolini, J. Nastoli, G. Bottelli, R. Folli and D. Cappelletti, Risk stratification in the long-QT sindrome, *N Engl J Med.*, May 8, vol.348(19):1866-74 (2003).

17. R. Rangayyan, *Biomedical Signal Analysis: a Case-Study Approach*, J. Wiley Inc. (2002).

18. G. Rizzo, M.C. Gilardi, A. Prinster, G. Lucignani, V. Bettinardi, F. Triulzi, A. Cardaioli, S. Cerutti and F. Fazio, A bioimaging integration system implemented for neurological applications, *J Nucl Biol Med.*, vol.38(4):579-85 (1994).

19. G. Rizzo, P. Scifo, M.C. Gilardi, V. Bettinardi, F. Grassi, S. Cerutti and F. Fazio, Matching a computerized brain atlas to multimodal medical images, *Neuroimage*, vol.6(1):59-69 (1997).

20. Y. Rudy, From Genome to Physiome: integrative models of cardiac excitation, *Ann. Biom. Engineer*, vol 28: 945-950 (2000).
21. M. Schroeder, *Fractals, chaos, power laws*, W.H. Freeman and Co, New York City, NY, USA (1991).
22. M.G. Signorini and S. Cerutti, Bifurcation analysis of a physiological model of the baroreceptive control, In: *Frontiers of Blood Pressure and Heart Rate analysis,* Di Rienzo et al eds., IOS Press, Amsterdam, pp. 29-43 (1997).
23. Task Force of the European Society of Cardiology and the North American Society of Pacing and Electrophysiology, Heart rate variability. Standards of measurement, physiological interpretation and clinical use. *Circulation*, n.93:1043-65 (1996).
24. W.J. Tompkins, *Biomedical Digital Signal Processing*, Prentice Hall, NJ (1995).
25. J.G. Webster, *Medical Instrumentation: Application and Design*, III Edition, Houghton Mifflin Co, Boston (1998).
26. B.J. West, *Fractal physiology and chaos in medicine*, World Scient.Publ. Co. Pte. Ltd (1990).

THE BINDING PROBLEM
AND THE EMERGENCE OF PERCEPTUAL MEANING

ELIANO PESSA

Dipartimento di Psicologia, Università di Pavia
Piazza Botta 6, 27100 Pavia, Italy

The binding problem stems from our difficulty in understanding how the brain is able to integrate different features, associated to the outputs of different detectors, into the unitary perception of a whole object. We analyze critically the claim that binding is produced by a synchronization of neural oscillations. To this regard we evidence how this proposal is untenable in its original form. We underline, however, that a suitable modification of it, taking into account the quantum nature of physical processes occurring within the brain, can open the way toward a more realistic solution of binding problem and a better explanation of most phenomena evidenced by psychology of visual perception.

1. Introduction

The expression *Binding Problem* (BP) refers to a whole class of seemingly different problems. It includes the *perceptual* BP, which is the problem of understanding how it occurs that different features are integrated within the global perception of a whole pattern, and the *cognitive* BP, which is the problem of understanding how different attributes, both of conceptual and of perceptual-motor nature, can be linked within the unified representation of a component of knowledge. In this chapter we will deal only with perceptual BP, even if the conclusions of our analysis could apply, through suitable adjustments, even to cognitive BP.

As regards perceptual BP we recall that, while generally it is viewed only as a problem for model builders and people takes as granted that our visual system has already solved it in an efficient way, there is some psychophysical evidence of the fact that sometimes the latter circumstance doesn't occur. Namely a conspicuous body of experimental findings (for a review see [81]) revealed that in some cases our visual system is unable to bind the features to objects in a correct way. An example is given by the so-called *illusory conjunctions*, in which perceptual features are unbound from the objects to which they were originally associated and can be recombined to form a new object [69] [70]. However here we will limit ourselves to deal with the problem of building reliable and biologically grounded models of the mechanisms responsible for visual binding.

Within this context the BP as such arose from the observation that an architecture made by a hierarchical arrangement of neuronal layers (supposed to underlie the processing of visual information within the brain) would be unable to account for the features of visual binding, as evidenced both by psychological research and by everyday perceptual experience. This is due to two main reasons:

a)   the number of inter-layer connections, required to produce all different kinds of possible feature conjunctions occurring within ordinary visual experience, would be practically unlimited and, in any case, far greater than the one of synaptic connections really present within the human brain;

b)   it would be impossible to explain how, in some cases, we are able to perceive without effort the existence of a given kind of feature conjunction without necessarily being able to detect the features themselves; a typical example is given by conjunctions implemented through the usual spatial relationships such as *to the right of*, *to the left of*, *over*, *under*, and so on; whereas we immediately perceive that, for instance, a chair is located to the right of a table, we are equally able to immediately perceive that an object A is located to the right of another object B, even if we are unable to detect the true nature of both A and B, as the latter have never been encountered before; no distribution of connection weights could support such an ability [25].

A number of different proposals have been made in order to overcome these difficulties, while continuing to adopt a neural network based framework. Within this chapter we will shortly review the advantages and the shortcomings of the main ones and such a synthetic analysis will lead us to argument against the impossibility of solving BP within a modeling context making use only of a system of interconnected neurons following deterministic updating rules. We will, then, propose, to deal with BP, an alternative framework, taking into account the probably quantum nature of the interaction of neurons with their surrounding medium.

2.   Hierarchical Feedforward Models

A prominent feature of human brain consists in its high speed in performing visual recognition tasks. For instance the data reported by Thorpe *et al.* [66] evidence how the visual processing in an object detection task within complex visual scenes takes a time of the order of 150 ms. This circumstance, as well as the findings evidencing an overall trend of increase of feature complexity and receptive field size along the ventral visual stream in macaque [36], led to the formulation of models of object recognition making use of hierarchical architectures based on layers of neuronal units interconnected only through feedforward connections. Among these models perhaps the most developed one was proposed by Riesenhuber and Poggio [53] [54]. The latter consists in a hierarchical arrangement of two kinds of cell layers: the ones containing only the so-called S-cells, that is filter cells associated to suitable receptive fields and sensitive to given features, and the ones containing only C-cells, that is pooling cells receiving inputs from suitable subsets of S-cells. Here the nomenclature adopted for the two kinds of cells follows the one already proposed by Fukushima [15].

Within the Riesenhuber-Poggio model the two layers alternate: the retina sends its output to S1 layer, which in turn sends its output to C1 layer. The latter, then, sends its output to the next S2 layer, and so on. The current implementation of this model includes, besides the retina, five successive cell layers: S1, C1, S2, C2 and a top layer containing view-tuned units (VTU). The S-cells, as well as the cells belonging to the top layer, have typically Gaussian transfer functions. Their receptive fields are chosen so as to be tuned to different orientations, specific of the single cells. As regards the C-cells their pooling function is the so-called MAX function. This means that the output of every C-cell is determined by the strongest afferent. This choice grants for a position-invariant detection of pattern features. A fully invariant object recognition (that is independent from rotations and scale transformations) is, then, obtained, by sending the outputs of the VTU to the hidden layer of a Gaussian Radial Basis Function (GRBF) network. Each one of the GRBF units belonging to this layer is associated to a particular prototype consisting of a particular view of the object to be recognized. As it is well known, if we shortly denote by p_i the prototype image associated to the i-th GRBF hidden unit and by x_i the input pattern, the output of this unit will be given by:

$$h_i = \{exp[-(P_i/\sigma_i)^2]\}/ (\Sigma_k \{exp[-(P_k/\sigma_k)^2]\}) , \qquad (1)$$

where σ_i is the 'variance' associated to the unit and P_i is a measure of the distance between p_i and x_i. Moreover, the output of this hidden layer is, in turn, sent to an output layer, generally including linear units, each one giving as output a specific recognition answer. The weights of the feedforward connections from the hidden to the output layer are, then, determined through a suitable supervised learning procedure based on the iterated presentation of suitable pairs, each made by an input stimulus and the associated correct recognition answer.

The simulations so far done evidenced a very good performance of this model in invariant recognition tasks, mainly in the ones requiring face recognition. Besides, the model seems to avoid the catastrophic increase of the number of units required to do these tasks. It, however, fails to account for some observed characteristics of human object recognition, which can be listed as follows:

1) human object recognition is not always invariant; for instance it is sensitive to rotations in the picture plane (see, e.g., [33], [42], [64]);

2) human visual system explicitly represents object parts in terms of their
    spatial relations and the latter are in turn represented independently of the
    parts they relate [26] [56] [57].

These circumstances seem to suggest that human subjects recognize objects
on the basis of some forms of *structural descriptions* of them, as already
hypothesized by researchers such as Biederman [4]. The ability to produce such
descriptions, however, cannot be learned in a supervised way. Namely this kind
of learning depends crucially on the presentation of a set of input-output pairs,
each one referred to specific instances. We can, thus, by presenting examples of
books lying on tables, induce a neural network to detect whether a book is lying
on a table or not. But, just because this kind of learning is always based on the
presentation of specific instances, it will be impossible, in principle, to induce a
neural network to detect whether an unknown object is or not lying on another
unknown object. Therefore our previous neural network, when receiving as
input a visual scene in which a man is sitting on a chair, will be unable to
correctly detect the presence of the spatial relationship *on*. The key point is that,
whatever be the extension of the training set, it will never allow for the ability to
abstract general spatial relationships, in a way independent of their arguments,
starting only from a finite number of concrete examples.

Once admitted the need for modeling the ability to do structural
descriptions, it follows that any model of this kind should perform, on every
input visual pattern, two different operations: a *segmentation* of the pattern into
its constituent parts (for instance the book and the table), and a *binding* of these
parts one to another, mediated by the binding of each part to a specific
relationship (for instance the book is bound to the relationship *on*). As regards
the latter operation we can distinguish between a *static* and a *dynamic* binding.
The former corresponds to the case in which the occurrence of each association
between a part and a spatial relationship, or between two parts and a spatial
relationship, is detected by a pre-dedicated unit. On the contrary, in a dynamic
binding each unit can be used to represent many different combinations, and its
role can change with time.

Models relying on static binding suffer from a catastrophic increase of the
number of units needed to detect all possible combinations associated to spatial
relationships occurring in realistic cases. Let us assume, for instance, that every
part of an object can be identified with a particular kind of elementary
component (a *geon* in Biederman's theory of recognition by components; see
[4]) and the total number of these different components be n. If we denote by m
the total number of different possible kinds of spatial relationships between two
elementary components, we will have that the total number of different possible
bindings between two different parts will be given by $n^2 m$. Let us now suppose
that, on the average, an object can be decomposed into k different parts. As its

structural description must take into account all possible pairings between different couples of parts, we will immediately obtain that the total number of different possible structural descriptions will be $s = k^2\,n^2\,m$. Now, to recognize the nature of a given object through a set of pre-dedicated cells, we will need a different recognizing unit for each possible Boolean function of these s different possibilities, as each function of this kind will code the structural description of a particular object. It is easy to see that the total number of these functions, and whence of recognizing units, is 2^s. What are the values of these quantities in realistic cases? If, to make a simple example, we take, following Biederman, $n=36$ and we choose (a strong underestimate) $k=2$, $m=4$, we will readily obtain that $s=20736$ and $2^s=2^{20736} \approx 10^{6500}$, a number far greater than the one of neurons in human brain!

This argument (and similar ones) rules out any possibility of resorting only to static binding. As regards dynamic binding, the problem is to individuate a neural mechanism implementing it. Most people proposed to identify this sort of binding with the synchrony between the activations of different units, or groups of units. In the next section we will explore the advantages and the shortcomings of this idea.

3. Binding through Synchrony

A synchrony between neuronal activations associated to visual activity has been observed in a number of experiments (see, e.g., [12] [18] [37] [39] [55] [61] [62]). Other experiments, however, didn't detect such a synchrony [41]. On the other hand, there is a conspicuous body of evidence regarding the ubiquitous nature of synchronization phenomena in human brain (see, for example, [5] [62]). Anyway, all these findings leave unanswered the question of the mechanism responsible for the observed synchrony. The theoretical hypotheses so far advanced can be listed as follows:

h.1) synchrony depends on the existence of suitable *delays* between the firings of different neurons located in different positions;

h.2) synchrony is due to the coupling between the activities of suitable *neural oscillators*;

h.3) synchrony is due to noise affecting the activities of coupled *neural oscillators*;

h.4) synchrony results from suitable features of neural firing dynamics;

h.5) synchrony results from the interactions of *chaotic neurons*;

h.6) synchrony is due to the effect produced on firing dynamics by force fields (of electromagnetic nature) present in extracellular medium.

We will now shortly discuss in this section the shortcomings of the first two proposals, delaying to the next section a synthetic review of the possibilities offered by the other ones.

3.1. *Synchrony by Delays*

This hypothesis states that a suitable distribution of time delays associated to the propagation of activation from a neuron to another along the connection lines can give rise, in short time, to a synchronization of firings of neurons belonging to a given group or of firings of two different neuronal groups. It is very popular and was used in a number of interesting models of perceptual binding, such as the ones by Hummel and Biederman [25], Hummel and Stankiewicz [24] [26] [27], Tononi *et al.* [68].

Of course, the right distribution of time delays is achieved, in turn, by postulating a suitable distribution of connection weights. When, however, this distribution doesn't coincide with the right one, the synchrony disappears, as evidenced by a number of mathematical studies (see, e.g., [8]). This occurs, in particular, when we exclude long-range connections and the distribution of connection weight values is disordered, circumstances which are similar to the ones characterizing biological brains. On the other hand, even very simple arguments show, in the case of toy models, that it is very implausible that a neural network can support a stable synchronization of the activities of its units. Let us consider, for instance, a ring of neurons, in which each neuron can be connected only to its two immediate neighbors. We will further suppose that all connection weights have random values, which can be positive or negative but whose absolute value is far lesser than 1. The dynamics of the *i*-th neuron will be described by a differential equation like the one fulfilled by McCulloch-Pitts neurons, that is:

$$dx_i/dt = -x_i + F(w_{i,i-1}x_{i-1} + w_{i,i+1}x_{i+1}) \tag{2}$$

where F is a sigmoidal function given by:

$$F(y) = 1/[1 + exp(-y)] \tag{3}$$

We can look for the equilibrium points of this dynamics, which are solutions of the system of equations:

$$-x_i + F(w_{i,i-1}x_{i-1} + w_{i,i+1}x_{i+1}) = 0 \tag{4}$$

If we take into account the smallness of absolute values of connection weights and we suppose that all activations be very small and close to zero, we can substitute the sigmoidal function with its linear approximation around $F(0)$.

Thus the previous nonlinear system becomes, in a first approximation, a linear algebraic system. By looking at the form of its coefficients matrix, it can be shown (we will omit here the details of the algebraic arguments) that this system admit one and only one solution provided that, for every value of the index i, the following inequality be satisfied:

$$1 - w_{i,i+1}\, w_{i+1,\,i} - w_{i,i-1}\, w_{i-1,i} \neq 0 \qquad (5)$$

It is easy to see that the latter is trivially satisfied, owing to the hypothesis introduced above on the smallness of absolute values of connection weights. We can, thus, conclude that our network has a unique equilibrium state, provided that the adopted approximation continue to be valid. It is, then, also possible to prove that this equilibrium state is *linearly stable*. Namely, if we denote by ξ_i a small perturbation of the equilibrium value of the activity of i-th neuron, straightforward manipulations show that, in a linear approximation, its time evolution is driven by the equation:

$$d\xi_i/dt = -\,\xi_i + F(x_v)\,[1 - F(x_v)]\,\xi_i \qquad (6)$$

where x_v denotes the value of the argument of the function F in correspondence to the equilibrium state. As the maximum possible value of $F(x_v)$ is ½, we are forced to conclude that the time evolution of ξ_i consists in an exponential decay towards the zero value. This assures the stability of equilibrium state.

The final conclusion of this argument is that this network cannot support a stable synchronization of neuronal activities, which could manifest itself only as a correlation between the time evolutions (for instance, of oscillatory type) of different neurons. Namely such time evolutions cannot exist as, owing to the stability of the equilibrium state, every external input gives rise only to a transient which quickly decays towards this state. Even a periodic input fails to induce synchronized oscillations as, owing to the smallness of connection weight values, it produces an effect only on the neuron to which it is directly applied, while this effect cannot be propagated to neighboring neurons. These conclusions, as expected, agree with the outputs of computer simulations of time evolution of such kind of networks.

These difficulties induced authors such as Gray [18] and Von der Malsburg [78] to restrict the role of synchrony only to pre-attentive processes in the lower areas of the visual cortex. In any case, most people believes that models based only on delays are insufficient to account for observed synchrony and that the latter can be explained only by resorting to networks including, already from the starting, neural oscillators.

3.2. *Synchrony by Coupling of Neural Oscillators*

In this case the synchrony refers to behaviors of suitable neural oscillators, already existing and constituting the basic elements of the neural network taken into consideration. It is hypothesized that each neural oscillator be characterized by its intrinsic frequency and that, once the different oscillators are coupled together, this coupling can enable an equalization of their frequencies, allowing for the eventual existence of constant phase shifts between them. Such an hypothesis is suggested by the fact that synchronized oscillatory activity has often been observed in the somatosensory system (see, e.g., [45] [63]) and in visual system [46].

The concrete model implementation of this hypothesis requires the specification of both the structure of a neural oscillator and the kind of coupling. To this regard, many choices are possible. Among the neural oscillators, probably one of most popular choices is the so-called *Wilson-Cowan oscillator*, consisting in a system of two neurons, one excitatory and the other inhibitory. The excitatory neuron sends an excitatory synaptic connection to the inhibitory neuron which, in turn, sends back an inhibitory connection to the excitatory neuron (see Figure 1). In some cases to the inhibitory neuron is added another inhibitory self-connection.

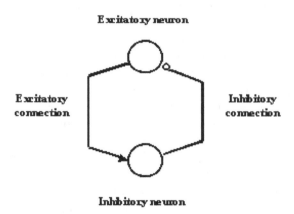

Figure 1. A model of a neural oscillator.

The dynamical equations describing the activity of this system can be cast under the form:

$$dx/dt = -x + F_\lambda(x - \beta y - \theta_e + I) \quad , \quad \tau\, dy/dt = -y + F_\lambda(\alpha x - \theta_i) \quad (7)$$

where x and y denote the output activity, respectively, of the excitatory and of the inhibitory neuron. Moreover α is the strength of the excitatory connection, whereas β is the one of inhibitory connection; θ_e and θ_i are the thresholds of excitatory and of inhibitory neuron, I denotes a generic external input (coming from the outside or from other oscillators) and τ is a suitable time constant characterizing the dynamics of the inhibitory neuron. Finally F_λ denotes the following generalization of the usual sigmoidal function:

$$F_\lambda(z) = = 1/[1 + exp(- z/\lambda)] \tag{8}$$

At first sight this description of a neural oscillator can appear as somewhat artificial and devoid of any biological plausibility. However it was shown that it can be derived from a suitable mean field approximation of the stochastic dynamics of a network of, undoubtedly more realistic, threshold neurons [6]. In any case, such a neural oscillator model is very convenient from a mathematical point of view. Namely it can be proved (see, e.g., [79]) that, by adopting suitable choices of model parameter values, the above dynamical system, in absence of external inputs, is *self-oscillating*, that is allows for the existence of a stable self-sustained oscillation (a so-called *limit cycle*) whose frequency depends on these values. However, to observe the occurrence of such a phenomenon, we need to start from a nonzero value of x, which can be obtained only by resorting to an external input. We can thus also say that this system begins to oscillate as a response to an outside signal. Computer simulations of this model show indeed that this is the case and that, owing to a number of reasons, the amplitude of the signal allowing for this effect must lie within a given interval: not too small nor too big.

We remark, however, that a number of studies preferred to use, instead of this model, a more abstract one, in which a neural oscillator is simply described through two variables: its *amplitude* $r(t)$ and its *phase* $\varphi(t)$. In the case in which the amplitude can be considered as nearly constant (for instance when the coupling with other oscillators or with the external environment is very weak and the system reached the limit cycle condition), the dynamical description of the oscillator reduces only to description of its phase dynamics. The latter, in the case of the i-th oscillator, can be cast under the general form:

$$d\varphi_i/dt = f_i(\varphi_i, s_1, \ldots, s_N) + \varepsilon \Sigma_j r_{ij}(\varphi_i, \varphi_j) \tag{9}$$

Here the auxiliary variables $s_1, \ldots, s_N$ (N is the total number of oscillators) have been introduced to describe the velocity of propagation of the influence produced by the phase of other oscillators on the oscillator under consideration. Namely these variables fulfill the differential equations:

$$ds_i /dt = \eta\, g_i\, (\varphi_i\, ,\, s_i\,) \qquad (10)$$

On the contrary the functions r_{ij} describe a direct coupling between oscillator pairs, producing instantaneous effects. The explicit forms chosen for the functions f_i, g_i and r_{ij} specify the model adopted to describe oscillator interactions. Moreover, the values of parameters ε and η characterize the kind of coupling model. When ε is vary small, far lesser than 1, we speak of *weakly coupled* oscillators, whereas, when η is very small, we speak of *slowly coupled* oscillators. These two features can, of course, occur simultaneously within the same model.

Besides the distinction between these two kinds of couplings, we stress that another important distinction is the one between *global* and *local* couplings. In the former case each oscillator is connected to every other oscillator belonging to the network, whereas in the latter the connections exist only between spatially neighboring oscillators (provided, of course, we introduced a suitable definition of neighborhood). The models with global couplings are very popular and a number of investigations (see, e.g., [21] [29] [65] [67]) evidenced how, when their parameters lie within certain ranges and the functions defining the couplings have been chosen in a suitable way, they give rise to synchronization of activities of neural oscillators constituting them, both in the case of weak and of slow couplings. Such a circumstance has been used to build a number of models of visual binding (for instance [9] [20] [79], to quote only few of them) as well as a number of artificial visual recognition devices [22] [35] [40] [82]. The main problem with these models, despite their mathematical attractiveness, is that they are unable to account for the spatio-temporal properties of object features, while these properties, as already Gestalt Psychologists emphasized, are critical in determining what is actually perceived. Namely, if we present as input a scene containing two objects located in two different places, every neural oscillator activated by one of them will automatically excite in a synchronous way, owing to the presence of global connections, every other oscillator of the network, preventing thus from a segmentation of the scene in which different sets of oscillators are activated by different objects. Moreover, we cannot claim that a fully connected network of oscillators mimics the pattern of synaptic connections observed in human and animal brains. Namely in the latter (see, for a discussion, [1]) the axonal as well as the dendritic ranges have an extension which, even if highly variable, is often far smaller than the dimensions of the whole system. Even if a neuron makes a very high number of synaptic contacts with other neurons, most of them can be considered as lying within its spatial neighborhood. And, what's more, owing to the finite propagation velocity of the neural pulse, the spatial locations of the interconnected neurons have a capital importance in determining the resulting temporal activation pattern.

These arguments prompted some researchers to resort to models based only on local couplings between neural oscillators [38] [80]. It can be shown, however, that within a network of locally coupled Wilson-Cowan oscillators, synchronization can be achieved only if all local connections have equal weights. As such a condition seems highly implausible, these models incorporate a mechanism of weight dynamical equalization, based on a idea first proposed by Von der Malsburg in 1982, which appears to have a physiological ground [11]. In short, it is hypothesized that every pair of neighboring oscillators be connected by two different kinds of synapses: the *permanent* one T_{ij} and the *dynamical* one J_{ij}. Whereas the permanent synapses are genetically given and cannot be modified, the dynamical ones change as a consequence of learning induced by momentarily activation patterns of network oscillators. Moreover, while all permanent synapses have the same weight and connect only immediately neighboring oscillators, the learning law fulfilled by dynamical synapses depends on the weight of permanent synapses and operates in two steps: an updating based on a suitable generalization of Hebbian law:

$$\Delta J_{ij} = \delta\, T_{ij}\, h(x_i)\, h(x_j) \tag{11}$$

followed by a normalization of the updated dynamical weights:

$$\hat{J}_{ij} = [\gamma\,(J_{ij} + \Delta J_{ij})]/[\varepsilon + \Sigma_k\,(J_{ik} + \Delta J_{ik})] \tag{12}$$

Here γ, δ and ε are suitable parameters, whereas the function $h(x)$ is defined by:

$$h(x) = 1 \ \text{ if } <x> \text{ is greater than } \theta, \ h(x) = 0 \ \text{ otherwise} \tag{13}$$

The symbol θ denotes a suitable threshold value, while $<x>$ is the temporal average of x over a suitable time interval.

It is possible to show that, given a right choice of model parameter values, such a mechanism induces in short time an equalization of connection weights and therefore allows for a synchronization of oscillators. It must, however, be complemented by another mechanism for inducing desynchronization, in order to avoid a synchronization between sets of oscillators excited by different parts of the same scene and corresponding to different objects. The most popular choice, to this regard, consists in introducing a *global inhibitor*, which receives inputs from every oscillator belonging to the network and sends, in turn, its inhibitory output to every one of them. Simulation results evidence how this mechanism could, in principle, account for the previously quoted experimental data on synchronization phenomena occurring in visual cortex and, at the same time, be successfully used in designing artificial image segmentation devices [10].

The main difficulty with this kind of models is the lack of proofs of their biological or cognitive plausibility. There exist, instead, arguments evidencing how weight normalization mechanism could be incompatible with the perceptual phenomenology experienced by human subjects as well as with the data on classical conditioning. Among these arguments the most effective one was proposed by Grossberg already in the Seventies [19]. It deals with a situation in which we have time changes in the structure of the input visual scene. Let us consider, for instance, a simple network containing three detecting units (or oscillators: the implementation doesn't matter), one detecting the presence of a square, another detecting the presence of a triangle and the third detecting the presence of a circle, and two recognizing units, one detecting that there is a triangle above a square and another detecting that there is a triangle under a circle (Figure 2).

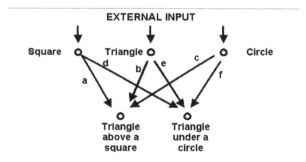

Figure 2. A small recognition network showing the inadequacy of normalization mechanism.

Let us further denote the weights of input connections to the first recognizing unit by a, b, c and the ones of input connections to the second recognizing unit by d, e, f. The normalization mechanism will force these weights to fulfill the general relationship:

$$a + b + c = d + e + f = \text{constant} \tag{14}$$

If now we present as input a visual scene in which we have a triangle above a square (Figure 3a) the recognizing unit "triangle above a square" will activate owing to the fact that a previous learning based on Hebbian mechanism raised the values of a, b. As a consequence, owing to the relationship written above,

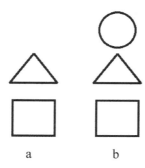

a   b

Figure 3. The two scenes used in evidencing the effects of normalization mechanism.

the value of c will be very small. But the same relationship will hold even for the connection weights of the other unit "triangle under a circle", which we suppose not to be activated, owing to the fact that no circle is present within the scene depicted in Figure 3a. Thus at least one of d, e, f should be associated to a high value and we can reasonably suppose that this will occur for e, f, being the weight of connections coming from the units detecting a triangle and a circle, which we can think of as still determined by previous learning.

Now, what will happen if our scene will change (Figure 3b) and, without removing the square, a circle staying above the triangle will appear? Of course the unit "triangle under a circle" will be activated, but, as even the other unit "triangle above a square" continues to be activated, just the Hebbian mechanism will produce a raise of the value of c, the weight of connection coming to this unit from the unit detecting the presence of a circle (now occurring within the scene). But the normalizing mechanism implies that a raise of c will be associated to an unavoidable decrease of a, b. Now, if we remove the circle, leaving again only the triangle above a square, this will automatically imply that the unit "triangle above a square" will not be activated (despite the presence both of the triangle and of the square), owing to the smallness of the weights a, b. Such a circumstance, however, contradicts the usual phenomenology of visual experience. If a human subject recognizes the occurrence of a triangle above a square, such a recognition will not be altered by the occurrence of a circle above the triangle nor by the disappearing of this latter.

As a general conclusion of all previous arguments we can assert that all mechanisms so far proposed to ensure synchronization, and based on coupling in a suitable way neural oscillators, suffer from a number of shortcomings, that, in ultimate analysis, reduce to their low plausibility and to their inability in accounting for the known phenomenology of human visual experience. In the following section we will shortly review other mechanisms, proposed to grant for synchronization, which are based on features usually not taken into consideration by traditional neural network models.

4. Non-traditional Synchronization Mechanisms

4.1. *Synchrony Induced by Noise*

From a number of years it is well known that external noise can give rise, when introduced in an additive or, chiefly, in a multiplicative way to a deterministic system, to interesting and somewhat unexpected effects. Among the latter we can quote *noise-induced order* [23], *noise-induced phase transitions* [17] [72] and *stochastic resonance* [16]. Some mathematical studies evidenced that noise can also induce a synchronization between the activities of neurons responding to external stimulations [44] [47]. The rationale for these findings stems from the fact that noise operates in such a way as to reduce the subtle effects of dynamical complexity, which is just responsible for chaotic behaviors and for the lack of synchronization. At the same time, the introduction of noise in an otherwise deterministic system could induce correlations which would be absent in the dynamics generated by the original system itself. Of course, all these effects occur only in presence of suitable forms of model equations and of suitable parameter values. The determination of the latter should be the goal of a general theory of *stochastic dynamical systems* which, however, is far from being complete. Therefore most conclusions are still grounded only on observed outcomes of computer simulations and we often lack methods to assess their reliability. In any case, the resort to models incorporating noise seems to offer a more realistic way to deal with the problem of synchrony in neural systems.

4.2. *Synchrony Induced by Features of Neural Firing Dynamics*

This topic has been dealt with by very few people. Whereas there is an intense debate about the best model of neural firing dynamics (see, for instance, [28]), it rarely touches the question of synchronization. Among the few researchers which proposed a modification of the usual models of this kind, in order to grant for synchronization, we will quote Sato [58]. It introduced a variant of the most popular model, the so-called *integrate-and-fire* neuron, in which, once membrane potential crossed the threshold value, it suddenly jumps to a value higher than firing threshold and starts a decrease toward a second threshold value (higher than firing threshold). Once reached the latter, the membrane potential jumps suddenly to zero. Sato was able to show that two interconnected neurons of this kind can synchronize their activities provided that their synaptic couplings fulfill suitable conditions. It is difficult to assess the relevance of these arguments for large networks containing many interconnected neurons.

We cannot, however, exclude that some features of neural firing dynamics be, at least partially, responsible for the synchronization observed in biological networks.

4.3. *Synchrony as a Byproduct of the Interactions of Chaotic Neurons*

The resort to deterministic chaos was stimulated by the discovery, made in the early Nineties, that within lattices of coupled chaotic maps it is possible to observe a global synchronization of individual map activities, provided that model parameter values lie within suitable intervals [34] [50]. The relevance of this fact for neural network models was acknowledged when people connected it to the observation, already made in the middle Eighties, that biological neurons can exhibit chaotic behaviors [2]. We underline that networks of chaotic maps are used more for designing artificial devices for perceptual segmentation, as in the model of van Leeuwen *et al.* [74], rather than to account for the behavior of biological neurons. However Jiang *et al.* [31] recently obtained precise conditions granting for the synchronization of output activities of chaotic neuron pairs. This work is awaiting for an extension to networks of coupled chaotic neurons. We remark here that deterministic chaos plays, in this context, a role opposite to the one of noise: while the latter represents the absence of any order and of any complexity, the former is associated to an excessive amount of complexity (which prevents from forecasting chaotic deterministic behaviors). Such a circumstance implies, in turn, an extreme sensitivity of chaotic systems to external inputs which, in given situations, can act so as destroy the deterministic chaos itself, leaving the place to ordered behaviors, such as synchronized oscillations. This, in ultimate analysis, is the nature of mechanism which could generate the synchrony as a byproduct of chaos. Not all researchers, however, agree on the relevance of deterministic chaos for modeling biological networks [14], claiming that it is nothing but an invention of mathematicians, devoid of any biological meaning.

4.4. *Synchrony due to Force Fields and to Non-Synaptic Interactions*

There is some evidence of the fact that neurons communicate not only through synapses but even through the extracellular electromagnetic field induced by the electrical activity of neurons themselves [30] [75]. Usually the phenomenon of modulation of single neuron firing by the firing of adjacent neurons is referred to as *ephaptic* transmission and was advocated to account for very fast neuronal firing synchronization observed in hippocampal slices *in vitro* [7]. Despite the fact that these phenomena are still poorly understood, they appear as potentially responsible for most collective behaviors observed in biological networks and a number of researchers claimed that a full solution of binding problem and a complete theory of consciousness should be based on a description of brain electromagnetic field features [43]. In fact, some simple neural network models evidenced that the inclusion of non-synaptic interactions, describing ephaptic couplings, induced a marked increase of the degree of synchronization between neuron activities [3]. However these findings were obtained only through computer simulations and the mechanism by which the electromagnetic field should induce a synchronization is still unclear.

To summarize, all non-traditional synchronization mechanisms presented in this section work (and perhaps more efficiently than traditional ones) if and only if we are, already from starting, in presence of a suitable *coherence-inducing* process, giving rise just to the conditions allowing for an optimal operation of the mechanisms themselves. In the next section we will introduce some hypotheses on these processes, based on an entirely new framework for dealing with emergence of cognitive abilities within biological matter.

5.   The Emergence of Perceptual Meaning

After reviewing the tremendous effort so far done in searching for mechanisms granting for reliable synchronization mechanisms, we underline that a fundamental question remains unanswered: why should we resort to synchronization when, even if we could justify its existence, it cannot, in principle, account for most features of human visual perception, as evidenced by laboratory experiments and everyday experience? To this regard we will remark that:

c.1)   the information which, in principle, can be extracted from a code based on synchrony is small and, in any case, smaller than the one which can be extracted from a code based on firing rate modulation [48] [52] [59];

c.2)   the synchronization cannot produce any effect in absence of suitable detectors of synchrony, which interpret its occurrence and use this interpretation to associate a meaning to the perceived pattern.

While the circumstance c.1) cannot be circumvented, a possible solution to the problem posed by c.2) consists in supposing that the brain doesn't need a module deputed to associate a meaning to every detected synchrony, as it suffices to associate to a network of synchrony detectors a set of connections pointing to effector units activating the correct behavioral responses to presented visual input patterns. It is easy to understand how such a solution implies that the assessment of usefulness of synchronization mechanism depends in a crucial way on its ability to generate the behaviors associated to an understanding of perceptual meaning of input patterns.

Once adopted such a perspective, it can easily proved that, except a number of simple cases, in most situations synchronization mechanisms are unable to generate such behaviors (for a deep discussion about this point see [73]). Let us make, to this regard, a simple example, based on scenes containing only two kinds of patterns: *triangles* and *square*. Moreover, only one kind of spatial relationship will be allowed: the one corresponding to the conjunction *above*. Let us further suppose that the detection of each pattern and of the occurrence of the spatial relationship be corresponding to the activation of a special unit, devoted to this task (we could, of course, imagine that the activation of each unit of this kind be nothing but an oversimplified description of the synchronized activation of the units belonging to a particular cell assembly). Within this framework, if we have a scene in which there is a triangle above a square, this will give rise to a synchronized activation of the three units *triangle, square* and *above*. We can, at this point connect the outputs of these three units to a further coincidence detecting unit, which will activate if and only if the three units fire synchronously. Once introduced the latter unit, it is a simple matter to connect its output to suitable answer producing units in such a way that, when this unit fires, the question "which pattern is above the square?" can elicit in a suitable answering unit the output "the triangle".

This sort of mechanism seems to work without problems, as it is able to give rise to right answers to questions about the perceived scene, thus endowing the system with the abilities implied by an understanding of the perceptual meaning of the scene itself, without the need for postulating a special meaning detecting device. However, despite its attractiveness, it is immediate to recognize that such a mechanism doesn't work. Namely, if we present another scene in which a square is above a triangle, it will still give rise to the synchronous activation of the three units *triangle, square* and *above*. But this will again activate the coincidence detecting unit which, owing to the structure of its interconnections with answering units, will still elicit, once made the question "which pattern is above the square?", the same answer as before, that is "the triangle", which in this case is obviously false. In short, the synchronization mechanism is unable to give rise to the understanding of perceptual meaning of a visual scene, as it cannot distinguish a triangle above a square from a square above a triangle.

How to circumvent such a difficulty without resorting to a complex symbolic representation of the structure of a visual scene? To this regard we remark that the previous arguments entail that the hypothetical mechanism solving the binding problem should be endowed with two main features: the ability to give rise to *long-range* (or *medium-range*) *correlations* between different parts of a visual scene, and the ability to endow these correlations with a *non-symmetrical nature*. So far, these two features appear only in models of phase transitions based on Quantum Field Theory (QFT). We have here no space for describing what is QFT and so we will limit ourselves to spend few words on this subject, to stress its relevance for the solution of binding problem.

We will start by recalling that QFT is radically different from Quantum Mechanics (QM), dealing with systems constituted by a finite, and fixed, number of particles, contained within a finite, and fixed, volume of space. On the contrary, the basic entities of QFT are the *fields*, that is distributions of energy over the whole infinite space. The fact that, on one hand, these fields are defined by uncertain quantities and that, on the other hand, they are equivalent to systems associated to an infinite (and continuous) number of degrees of freedom entails that within QFT the same system can allow for different, *physically non-equivalent*, representations. Each representation can, thus, be identified with the description of a different *phase* of the system and we can therefore assert that only within QFT we can deal with *phase transitions*, that is qualitative structural changes of the system itself [60] [71].

The theory of phase transitions based on QFT identifies each transition with a phenomenon of *symmetry breaking* (SB), in which the system, while fulfilling laws whose form doesn't change with respect to symmetry transformations, chooses to lie in a particular ground state, which is no longer invariant with respect to these transformations. A typical example is given by the phase transition from the paramagnetic to the ferromagnetic state, in which, while the laws are invariant with respect to rotations in the three-dimensional space, the occurrence of the ferromagnetic state itself gives rise to a non-symmetric situation, owing to the presence of a preferred direction in space (the one of spontaneous magnetization of the sample). A remarkable feature, present only within QFT, is that, after a SB, every disturbance of the new ground state thus generated gives rise, in turn, to a back-reaction of the system itself, counteracting the disturbance and keeping unchanged this ground state. This feature is known as *generalized rigidity* and, in a first approximation, can be described as due to the action of suitable information carriers, appearing as a response to external disturbances, which constrain all system components to behave in a coherent way so as to keep unchanged the ground state quoted above. These information carriers, commonly named *Goldstone bosons*, are nothing but generators of long-range correlations, in turn inducing collective behaviors in the components of the system under study.

To summarize, QFT, and only it, gives rise to models endowed with both long-range correlations and SB, just the two features which we required for a solution of binding problem. It is therefore not surprising that, already from the Sixties, QFT have been used to model brain phenomena. In more recent years QFT-based models of behavior of biological matter gave rise to the so-called *Quantum Brain Theories* [32] [77], as well as to models of memory operation [51] [76]. We therefore propose to use QFT even to solve the binding problem, by resorting to the introduction of a suitable *attentional mechanism* (this point was recently stressed also by Hummel [24]). To this regard, let us first remark that there are two kinds of SB phenomena: the *intrinsic* (or *spontaneous*) and the *extrinsic* ones. While the former occur when a critical parameter crosses a given critical value (as it is the case for the temperature in the paramagnetic-ferromagnetic transition), the latter are induced by an explicit input action exerted from outside. If now we allow for a QFT-based description of the operation of visual system it follows that an attentional system, whose activity can be triggered both by external stimulation features or by inner expectations, can induce within this system an extrinsic SB leading simultaneously to both a long-range correlation between different parts of a scene and an asymmetry of the coherent structure thus created.

While avoiding a detailed discussion about how we could formulate a concrete model of the operation of visual system following these guidelines, we will stress that its QFT-based features should not necessarily be present at the level of neurons, but could characterize, instead, lower levels, such as the one of the interactions between the macromolecules embedded within the extracellular liquid. Without pursuing further this topic, we underline that this line of research appears, so far, the only one available to try to escape from the difficulties evidenced by all other solutions of binding problem.

6. Conclusions

The arguments introduced in this chapter lead to an unescapable conclusion: both proposed solutions of binding problem, the one based on feedforward architectures and the one based on synchronization of neuronal activity, are unable to reach their goal: that of accounting for the emergence of visual meaning, as observed in everyday experience and in laboratory experiments, through a resort to biologically plausible mechanisms. This doesn't entail that both solutions cannot account in a satisfactory way for particular, and limited, kinds of visual recognition. As a matter of fact, they actually play such a role with great ingenuity. We claim, however, that a general solution of binding problem will never attained on these grounds. To this regard, we proposed to resort to QFT for building new kinds of models of the operation of visual system, with the hope that these latter, owing to the unique features of QFT, be able to circumvent the difficulties encountered by previous models and discussed above. The concrete formulation of the new models seems to be a great challenge even for the most refined theoreticians, because of the mathematical difficulties inherent in the actual form of QFT. However, some recent findings about the equivalence between QFT and other more tractable theories [13] [49] let us hope that in short time most neural network model builders will easily integrate the new framework within their old schemata.

References

1. M.Abeles, *Corticonics*, Cambridge University Press (1991).
2. K.Aihara, G.Matsumoto and M.Ichikawa, *Physics Letters A* **111**, 251 (1985).
3. P.Aronsson and H.Liljenström, *BioSystems* **63**, 43 (2001).
4. I.Biederman, *Psychol. Rev.* **94**, 115 (1987).
5. S.L.Bressler and J.A.S.Kelso, *Trends in Cognitive Sciences* **5**, 26 (2001).
6. J.Buhmann, *Phys. Rev. A* **40**, 4145 (1989).
7. G.Buzsáki, Z.Horváth, R.Urioste, J.Hetke and K.Wise, *Science* **256**, 1025 (1992).
8. S.R.Campbell, D.L.Wang and C.Jayaprakash, *Neural Computation* **11**, 1595 (1999).
9. T.Chawanya, T.Aoyagi, I.Nishikawa, K.Okuda and Y.Kuramoto, *Biol. Cyb.* **68**, 483 (1993).
10. K.Chen, D.L.Wang and X.Liu, *IEEE Trans. Neural Networks* **11**, 1106 (2000).
11. F.Crick, *Proc. Natl. Acad. Sci. USA* **81**, 4586 (1984).
12. A.K.Engel, P.König and W.Singer, *Proc. Natl. Acad. Sci. USA* **88**, 9136 (1991).
13. H.C.Fogedby, *Phys. Rev. E* **57**, 49431 (1998).
14. W.J.Freeman, R.Kozma and P.J.Werbos, *BioSystems*, **59**, 109 (2001).
15. K.Fukushima, *Biol. Cyb.* **36**, 193 (1980).
16. L.Gammaitoni, P.Hänggi, P.Jung and F.Marchesini, *Rev. Mod. Phys.* **70**, 223 (1998).
17. J.García-Ojalvo and J.M.Sancho, *Noise in spatially extended systems*, Springer (1999).
18. C.M.Gray, *Neuron* **24**, 79 (1999).
19. S.Grossberg, *Biol. Cyb.* **21**, 145 (1976).
20. S.Grossberg and D.Somers, *Neural Networks* **4**, 453 (1991).
21. F.C.Hoppensteadt and E.M.Izhikevich, *Weakly Connected Neural Networks*, Springer (1997).
22. F.C.Hoppensteadt and E.M.Izhikevich, *IEEE Trans. Neural Networks* **11**, 734 (2000).
23. W.Horsthemke and R.Lefever, *Noise-induced Transitions*, Springer (1984).
24. J.E.Hummel, *Visual Cognition* **8**, 489 (2001).
25. J.E.Hummel and I.Biederman, *Psychol. Rev.* **99**, 480 (1992).
26. J.E.Hummel and B.J.Stankiewicz, An architecture for rapid, hierarchical structural description, in: T.Inui and J.McClelland (Eds.), *Attention and Performance XVI: Information Integration in Perception and Communication*, MIT Press (1996).
27. J.E.Hummel and B.J.Stankiewicz, *Spatial Vision* **10**, 201 (1996).
28. E.M.Izhikevich, *IEEE Trans. Neural Networks* **15**, 1063 (2004).

29. E.M.Izhikevich and F.C.Hoppensteadt, *SIAM J. Appl. Math.* **63**, 1935 (2003).
30. J.G.R.Jefferys, *Physiol. Rev.* **75**, 689 (1995).
31. W.Jiang, D.Bin and K.M.Tsang, *Chaos, Solitons and Fractals* **22**, 469 (2004).
32. M.Jibu and K.Yasue, *Quantum Brain Dynamics and Consciousness: An Introduction*, Benjamins (1995).
33. P. Jolicoeur, *Mind & Language* **5**, 387 (1990).
34. K.Kaneko, *Physica D* **41**, 137 (1990).
35. Y.Kazanovich and R.Borisyuk, *BioSystems* **67**, 193 (2002).
36. E.Kobatake and K.Tanaka, *J.Neurophys.* **71**, 856 (1994).
37. P.König, A.K.Engel and W.Singer, *Proc. Natl. Acad. Sci. USA* **92**, 290 (1995).
38. P.König and T.B.Schillen, *Neural Computation* **3**, 155 (1991).
39. A.K.Kreiter and W.Singer, *J. Neurosci.* **16**, 2381 (1996).
40. M.Kuzmina, E.Manykin and I.Surina, *BioSystems* **76**, 43 (2004).
41. V.A.F.Lamme and H.Spekreijse, *Nature* **396**, 362 (1999).
42. R.Lawson, *Acta Psychologica* **102**, 221 (1999).
43. J.McFadden, *Journal of Consciousness Studies* **9**, 23 (2002).
44. D.McMillen and N.Kopell, *Journal of Computational Neuroscience* **15**, 143 (2003).
45. V.N.Murthy and E.E.Fetz, *J. Neurophysiol.* **76**, 3968 (1996).
46. S.Neuenschwander and W.Singer, *Nature* **379**, 728 (1996).
47. K.Pakdaman and D.Mestivier, *Physica D* **192**, 123 (2004).
48. S.Panzeri and S.R.Schultz, *Neural Computation* **13**, 1311 (2001).
49. R.Pastor-Satorras and R.V.Solé, *Phys. Rev. E* **64**, 051909 (2001).
50. L.M.Pecora and T.L.Carroll, *Phys. Rev. Lett.* **64**, 821 (1990).
51. E.Pessa and G.Vitiello, *Mind and Matter* **1**, 59 (2004).
52. G.Pola, A.Thiele, K.-P.Hoffmann and S.Panzeri, *Network: Comput. Neural Syst.* **14**, 35 (2003).
53. M.Riesenhuber and T.Poggio, *Neuron* **24**, 87 (1999).
54. M.Riesenhuber and T.Poggio, *Nature Neuroscience* **11**, 1019 (1999).
55. E.Rodriguez, N.George, J.-P.Lachaux, J.Martinerie, B.Renault and F.J.Varela, *Nature* **397**, 430 (1999).
56. J.Saiki and J.E.Hummel, *J.Exp.Psychol.: Hum.Percept.Perform.* **24**, 227 (1998).
57. J.Saiki and J.E.Hummel, *Memory & Cognition* **26**, 1138 (1998).
58. Y.D.Sato, *Physics Letters A* **319**, 486 (2003).
59. S.R.Schultz, H.D.R.Golledge and S.Panzeri, Synchronization, binding and the role of correlated firing in fast information transmission, in: S.Wermter, J.Austin and D.Willshaw (Eds.), *Emergent Neural Computational Architectures Based on Neuroscience*, Springer (2000).
60. G.L.Sewell, *Quantum Theory of Collective Phenomena*, Oxford University Press (1986).

61. W.Singer, *Neuron* **24**, 49 (1999).
62. W.Singer and C.M.Gray, *Ann. Rev.Neurosci.* **18**, 555 (1995).
63. M.Steriade, F.Amzica and D.Contreras, *J. Neurosci.* **16**, 392 (1996).
64. M.J.Tarr and S.Pinker, *Psychological Science* **1**, 253 (1990).
65. P.Tass and H.Haken, *Biol. Cyb.* **74**, 31 (1996).
66. S.Thorpe, D.Fize and C.Marlot, *Nature* **381**, 520 (1996).
67. A.Tonnelier, S.Meignen, H.Bosch and J.Demongeot, *Neural Networks* **12**, 1213 (1999).
68. G.Tononi, O.Sporns and G.M.Edelman, *Cerebral Cortex* **2**, 310 (1992).
69. A. Treisman, *Philos. Trans. R. Soc. Lond.* **B353**, 1295 (1998).
70. A. Treisman and H. Schmidt, *Cogn. Psychol.* **14**, 107 (1982).
71. H.Umezawa, *Advanced Field Theory. Micro, Macro, and Thermal Physics*, American Institute of Physics (1993).
72. C.Van den Broeck, J.M.R.Parrondo and R.Toral, *Phys. Rev. Lett.* **73**, 3395 (1994).
73. F.Van der Velde and M.De Kamps, *Brain and Mind* **3**, 291 (2002).
74. C.van Leeuwen, M.Steyvers and M.Nooter, *J. Math. Psychol.* **41**, 319 (1997).
75. E.J.Vigmond, P.Velazquez, T.A.Valiante, B.L.Bardakjian and P.Carlen, *J. Neurophysiol.* **78**, 3107 (1997).
76. G.Vitiello, *International Journal of Modern Physics B* **9**, 973 (1995).
77. G.Vitiello, *My double unveiled*, Benjamins (2001).
78. C.Von der Malsburg, *Neuron* **24**, 95 (1999).
79. C.Von der Malsburg and J.Buhmann, *Biol. Cyb.* **67**, 233 (1992).
80. D.L.Wang and D.Terman, *IEEE Trans. Neural Networks* **6**, 283 (1995).
81. J.M.Wolfe and K.R.Cave, *Neuron* **24**, 11 (1999).
82. Y.Yamaguchi and H.Shimizu, *Neural Networks* **7**, 49 (1994).

SEQUENCE RULE MODELS FOR WEB USAGE MINING

PAOLA CERCHIELLO

Dipartimento di Statistica, Università degli Studi Milano-Bicocca
paolacerchiello@libero.it

PAOLO GIUDICI

Data Mining Laboratory, Università degli Studi di Pavia
giudici@unipv.it

Every time a user links up to a web site, the server keeps track of all the actions accomplished in a *log file*. What is captured is the "click flow" (clickstream) of the mouse and the keys used by the user during the navigation inside the site. Usually every click of the mouse corresponds to the viewing of a web page. Therefore, we can define the clickstream as the sequence of the web pages requested. The objective of this chapter is to show how web clickstream data can be used to understand the most likely paths of navigation in a web site, with the aim of predicting, possibly on-line, which pages will be seen, having seen a specific path of other pages before. Such analysis can be very useful to understand, for instance, what is the probability of seeing a page of interest (such as the buying page in an e-commerce site) coming from another page. Or what is the probability of entering (or exiting) the web site from any particular page. From a methodological viewpoint, our aim is to present new associative models, obtained by means of statistical graphical Markov models, and compare them with classical association rules, direct or embodied in classification tree models. More specifically, as web pages are ordered in time, we shall consider sequence rules.

1. Sequence Rules

We first briefly recall what a sequence rule is. For more details the reader can consult a recent text on data mining, such as Han and Kamber [4] or, from a more statistical viewpoint, Hand *et al.* [5], Hastie *et al.* [3] and Giudici [2].

An *association rule* is a statement between two sets of binary variables (itemsets) A and B, that can be written in the form A $\rightarrow$ B, to be interpreted as a logical statement: *if A, then B.* If the rule is ordered in time we have a sequence rule and, in this case, A preceeds B.

In web clickstream analysis (see e.g. [1]), a sequence rule is typically *indirect:* namely, between the visit of page A and the visit of page B other pages can be seen. On the other hand, in a *direct* sequence rule A and B are seen consecutively.

A sequence rule model is, essentially, an algorithm that searches for the most interesting rules in a database. In order to find a set of rules, statistical measures of "interestingness" have to be specified. The measures more commonly used in web mining to evaluate the importance of a sequence rule are the indexes of support and confidence.

In this chapter we shall consider mainly the confidence index. The confidence for the rule $A \rightarrow B$ is obtained dividing the number of server sessions which satisfy the rule by the number of sessions containing the page A. Therefore, the confidence approximates the conditional probability that, in a server session in which page A has been seen, page B is subsequently requested. We finally remark that classification trees represent a global model to obtain sequence rules (see e.g. Giudici [2]).

2. Graphical Models

A graphical model (see for example Lauritzen [6]) is a family of probability distributions incorporating the conditional independence assumptions represented by a graph. It is specified via a graph that depicts the local relations among the variables (that are represented with nodes). In this chapter we will focus on the case in which all considered variables are discrete, and the graph is undirected (symmetric). It is known that recursive graphical models consist of a powerful tool for predictive data mining, because of their fundamental assumption of probability dependency between variables. However, symmetric graphical models can be considered as an important and valid tool in the preliminary phase of analysis because they can show the main relevant association, useful to construct a subsequent recursive model.

3. Web Usage Mining

The data set that we consider to illustrate our methodology is the result of the elaboration of a log file concerning a site of e-commerce, described, for instance, in Giudici [2]. The whole data set contains 250711 observations, each corresponding to a click, that describe the navigation paths of 22527 visitors among the 36 pages which compose the site of the webshop. For illustrative purposes, Table 1 reports a very small extract of the available dataset, corresponding to the user session of one visitor.

Table 1. Extract of the considered dataset

c_value	c_time	c_caller
70ee683a6df...	14OCT97:11:09:01	home
70ee683a6df...	14OCT97:11:09:08	catalog
70ee683a6df...	14OCT97:11:09:14	program
70ee683a6df...	14OCT97:11:09:23	product
70ee683a6df...	14OCT97:11:09:24	program

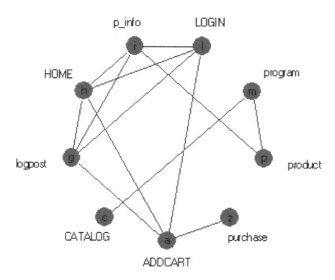

Figure 1. Graphical model with the variable 'purchase'.

In order to model the above data we have considered three main classes of statistical models: sequence rules, decision trees and symmetric graphical models. We underline that for the construction of the symmetric graphical models we have used the software MIM (www.hypergraph.com), instead for the association rules and the decision trees we have considered SAS Enterprise Miner.

We considered two contexts of analysis: in the first one, in order to obtain a useful comparison between graphical model and decision trees, we introduced a target variable 'purchase' that describes whether a client buys or not the products sold. A forward selection procedure, using a significance level of 5%, gave us the structure in Figure 1.

From Figure 1 the variable 'purchase' has only one link (one direct association), with the variable 'addcart'. In Figure 2 we compare this result with a classification tree model.

The decision tree in Figure 2 gives us a similar result, in fact 'addcart' represents the variable most important in the first split of the tree. Therefore we can conclude that graphical models and decision trees give consistent results.

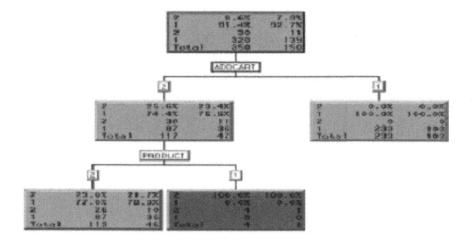

Figure 2. Decision tree with the variable 'purchase'.

In the second context of analysis we excluded the target variable 'purchase' in order to obtain a comparison between graphical models and sequence rule models. In order to summarise the main results of this analysis, in Figure 3 we present the selected undirected graphical model (according to a forward procedure and 5% significance level). Furthermore, we attach to each edge the highest of the two confidence indexes and conditional probabilities associated to it. For lack of space, in Figure 3 we represent such statistics only for the two strongest associations.

The graphical model in Figure 3 shows, as the strongest associations, the relationship between the variables catalog-program and program-product. We remark that, while confidence indexes are based on the results from the Apriori algorithm of SAS Enterprise Miner (see for instance Giudici [2]) conditional probabilities have been derived from the fitted contingency tables produced by the software MIM.

Comparing confidence indexes with conditional probabilities it turns out that the results from graphical models are quite similar with those from sequence rules. This means that, for this kind of data, sequence rules, based on marginal associations, constitute a valid approximation to detect association structures well described by a graphical model. On the other hand, they are much easier to calculate and interpret.

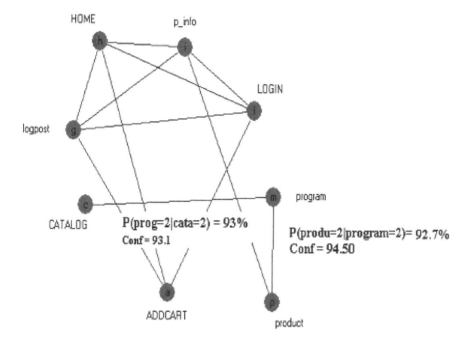

Figure 3. Graphical model with confidence indexes and conditional probabilities.

References

1. P. Giudici, Association models for web mining, *Atti della XLI riunione scientifica della Società Italiana di Statistica*, Cleup, Milano, pp. 329-338 (2002).
2. P. Giudici, *Applied Data mining, statistical methods for business and industr.* Wiley, London (2003).
3. T. Hastie, R. Tibshirani, and J. Friedman, *The elements of statistical learning: data mining, inference and prediction*, Springer-Verlag, Berlin (2001).
4. J. Han and M. Kamber, *Data mining: concepts and techniques*, Morgan Kaufman, New York (2001).
5. D.J. Hand, H. Mannilla, and P. Smyth, *Principles of Data Mining*, MIT Press, New York (2001).
6. S.L. Lauritzen, *Graphical models,* Oxford, Oxford University Press (1996).

AN IMPROVED 3D FACE RECOGNITION METHOD BASED ON NORMAL MAP

A. F. ABATE, M. NAPPI, S. RICCIARDI, G. SABATINO

Dipartimento di Matematica ed Informatica
Università di Salerno
84084 Fisciano (SA), Italy
Email: {abate, mnappi, sricciardi, gsabatino}@unisa.it

This chapter presents a face recognition method comparing a 3D facial model, to a gallery of previously enrolled faces. The geometrical features in the input mesh are represented by a bidimensional matrix, the normal map, storing local curvature data as the rgb components of a color image. The robustness of the proposed approach to facial expressions has been improved by a weighted mask automatically calculated for every subject in the gallery using a set of specific expressive variations. As comparison between normal maps is executed in a 2D space, the computational cost of this method is low. We present the results of our method on a 3d database of human faces, featuring different races, sex, ages, and expressions.

1. Introduction

The vast majority of face recognition methodologies are based on 2D image processing of photos or video footage offering the advantage of a simple and affordable data acquisition. They typically perform well when scene lighting, camera position and orientation are carefully controlled, but recognition becomes increasingly more difficult and unreliable when face position and orientation are not known or in case of strong variations in facial expression.

As tridimensional scanning techniques for face and full body are becoming more diffused and reliable, it is now possible to create detailed 3D facial database for biometrical purposes. This technology is pushing the development of recognition methods to fully exploits the potential of 3D face representation. Indeed, if the acquisition is performed correctly, the resulting surface of a 3D face model is more independent to lighting conditions, and even its position and orientation in 3D space respect a given reference system are much less problematic than in a 2D space [1].

This chapter presents a 3D face recognition method based on normal map [2], a bidimensional matrix representing local curvature data of a 3D polygonal model, aimed to biometrical applications. The proposed algorithm deliver a fast and accurate one-to-one/one-to-many face comparison working in a 2D space with improved robustness to facial expressions compared to previous works based on mesh normals [3].

This chapter is organized as follows. In Section 2 related works are presented. In Section 3 the proposed methodology is presented in detail. In Section 4 the results of the proposed methodology are presented and discussed. The chapter concludes in Section 5 showing directions for future research.

2. Related Works

The early researches on 3D face recognition were conducted over a decade ago as reported from Bowyer et al. [4] in their recent survey on this topic and many different approaches have been developed over time to address this challenging task. In most methods, before the recognition phase begins a face normalization is performed to recover the input data from orientation or scaling issues due to the acquisition process. To this aim some authors segment a range image based on principal curvature to find a plane of bilateral symmetry through the face [5], or more frequently a set of feature points is found (nose tips, eye contours, etc.) and then is used as a guide to standardize face pose [6] through a 3D transformation. In other cases a semiautomatic, interactive approach is adopted instead, manually selecting three or more feature points to calculate the orientation of face in 3D space.

The comparison between 3D facial representations can be performed according to different techniques and strategies. Indeed a first classification of 3D face recognition algorithms can be done based on their ability to work on neutral faces, i.e. faces showing a standard "relaxed" expression, or to cope with shape variations due to random facial expressions. To the first category belong methods based on feature extraction to describe both curvature and metric size properties of the face represented as a point in feature space and therefore measuring the distance to other points (faces) [7], or extensions to the range images of 2D face recognition techniques based on eigenface [8] or Hausdorff distance matching [9]. Other authors compare faces through a spherical correlation of their Extended Gaussian Image [10], through Principal Component Analysis (PCA) [11, 12], or even measure the distance between 3D face surfaces by the Iterative Closest Point (ICP) method [13].

To the aim of increase recognition rate in case of expression variations Bronstein et al. [14] apply an isometric transformation approach to 3D face analysis based on canonical images, while other authors combine 3D and 2D similarity scores obtained comparing 3D and 2D profiles [15], or extract a feature vector combining Gabor filter responses in 2D and point signatures in 3D [16].

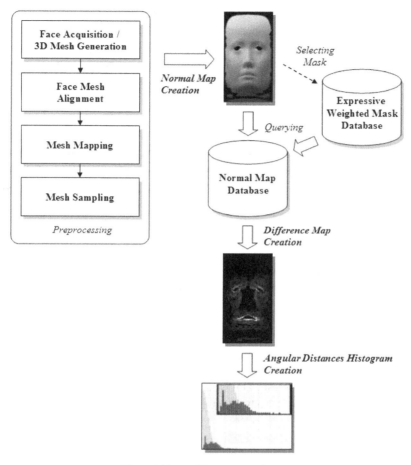

Figure 1. Recognition process scheme.

3. The Proposed Method

The basic idea of the proposed method is to represent the tridimensional face surface by a bidimensional matrix, the *normal map*, and then to search for a match measuring the distance between this map and the gallery maps in the reference database.

More precisely, we want to represent each normal vector of a 3D face mesh, by a pixel color, using the r,g,b pixel components to store the three vector components. To this aim we project the 3D geometry onto a 2D space through spherical mapping, thus obtaining a representation of original face geometry which retains spatial relationships between facial features. The comparison between two faces is therefore performed calculating the *difference map* between the corresponding normal map, weighted by a previously built *expressive weighted map.*

The whole recognition process is resumed in the schematic view showed in Figure 1 and discussed in depth in the following subsections 3.1. to 3.7.

3.1. *Face Acquisition*

One of the goals of the presented method is the ability to work on a polygonal face model regardless to its position, rotation or scaling within an absolute reference coordinate system during the acquisition process. While the mesh alignment task is explained in the next subsection, there are some general requisites the mesh have to meet to be registered in the reference database or to allow a valid comparison.

Indeed, the mesh should include a set of basic facial features such as both eyes, nose, mouth, forehead, chin. As the hair surface is not reliable to face recognition, it could and should not be included in the mesh.

There are not strict polygonal resolution requirements for the face model, and, while a good level of detail and a symmetrical mesh topology are preferable, they are not necessary for the system to work.

Any face scanning system such as laser scanners, structured light scanners and even image feature based mesh warping could produce valid 3D data for the presented method. As most 3D scanning systems produce range data, and therefore 3D polygonal mesh, almost unaffected from lighting conditions, this peculiarity turn out in a clear advantage for use in face recognition.

3.2. *Face Alignment*

Due to posing issues during the acquisition, the face mesh could be translated in any direction respect to the coordinate system origin. Additionally it could be arbitrarily scaled and rotated as well.

As the only data relevant to the proposed recognition method are the normals to each polygons in the face model, which measure the local curvature of the surface, we first calculate the mesh centroid and then, subtracting its coordinates (c_x, c_z, c_z) from each mesh vertex, we align the centroid and the whole mesh to the axis origin.

Scale factor of face mesh is simply not an issue as we normalize normal vector length before further processing.

To allow a coherent assignment of mapping coordinates as detailed in subsection 3.3., we need to know the orientation of face mesh in 3D space and eventually re-align it. Normalization of face mesh orientation in 3D space is achieved through a semi-automatic procedure.

First, three fiducial points with known spatial relationships are selected interactively on the face surface, then a rigid body transformation of vertex coordinates is performed to re-align the mesh. Valid fiducial points are the inner eye (left and right) and the nose tips, which are easily found on any face mesh and due to their peculiar local curvature could even be located automatically in a future version of this method.

3.3. Mesh Mapping

The shape information of a facial surface is "encoded" in its local curvature features which may be viewed as a digital signature of the face. This information in a polygonal mesh is given by the polygon normals. As we want to represent normal vectors by a color image while retaining spatial relationships in the 3D mesh, we first need to project each vertex coordinates onto a 2D space, a task referred as mapping.

We used a spherical projection (adapted to mesh dimension), because it fits better the actual 3D shape of the face mesh. More formally, given an arbitrary mesh M, we want associate to each mesh vertex v_i with coords $(x_i, y_i, z_i) \in R^3$ the ordered couple $(u_i, v_i) \in (U, V)$ with $0 \leq u, v \leq 1$. For each vertex v_i of mesh M, the formula is given by:

$$u_i = \phi\left(\arctan\left(\frac{x_i \cdot \frac{diamY}{diamX}}{z_i} \right) / 2\pi \right),$$

$$v_i = \left| \frac{1}{2} - \arctan\left(\frac{y_i}{\sqrt{x^2 + z^2}} \right) / \pi \right|$$

where *diamX* and *diamX* are the diameters of mesh M on Y and X axis respectively and $\phi(c)$ return the fractional part of the value c. The resulting face geometry of a generic face mesh, showed in Figure 2-a, projected onto the (U, V) domain is shown in Figure 2-b.

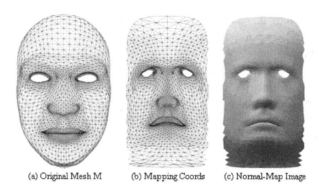

(a) Original Mesh M   (b) Mapping Coords   (c) Normal-Map Image

Figure 2. Normal map generation phases. Normal map is 24-bit $[n_x\ n_y\ n_z]$ visualized as $[r,\ g,\ b]$.

3.4. *Mesh Sampling*

Now it is possible to store normal data representing face geometry and topology in a bidimensional matrix N with dimension $k \times l$. To this purpose we have to sample the mapped geometry to quantize the length of the three versors of each normal.

So we can assign to each pixel in N, the normal components $[n_x, n_y, n_z]$ to correspondent surface region given by the mapping coordinates (u, v) of the polygons (i.e. the mapping coordinates of the triangles vertices if M a tri-mesh) and, as the matrix N has discrete dimensions, the resulting sampling resolution for the mesh is $1/k$ for ther u range and $1/l$ for the v range. The normal components $[n_x, n_y, n_z]$ are stored in N using a value belonging to the R,G,B color space. We refer to the resulting matrix N as the normal map of mesh M. A normal map with a standard color depth of 24 bit allows 8 bit quantization for each normal component, this precision proved to be adequate for the recognition process (Figure 2-c).

3.5. *Normal Map Comparison*

When the sampling phase is completed, we can register the new face, i.e. its normal map, in the reference database, or perform a search through it to find a matching subject.

The basic idea for estimate the comparison between any two face mesh M_A and M_B (namely their normal maps N_A and N_B) is achieved calculating the angle included between each pairs of pixel colors (in other words, the normals with corresponding mapping coordinates), and storing it in a new map D.

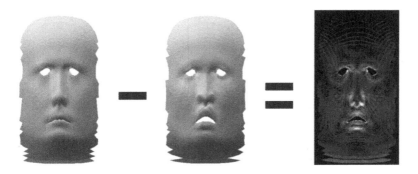

Figure 3. Example of comparison between two Normal Map 128×128. Difference Map (right) 128×128 is created from (left) and (center).

As each pixel (x_{N_A}, y_{N_A}) in N_A corresponding color components $(r_{N_A}, g_{N_A}, b_{N_A})$ and each pixel (x_{N_B}, y_{N_B}) in N_B has corresponding components $(r_{N_B}, g_{N_B}, b_{N_B})$ the angle included between the normals represented by each pair of pixel with $x_{N_A} = y_{N_A}$ and $x_{N_B} = y_{N_B}$ is given by:

$$\theta = \arccos \left(r_{N_A} \cdot r_{N_B} + g_{N_A} \cdot g_{N_B} + b_{N_A} \cdot b_{N_B} \right)$$

with components opportunely normalized from color domain to spatial domain, so $0 \leq r_{N_A}, g_{N_A}, b_{N_A} \leq 1$ and $0 \leq r_{N_B}, g_{N_B}, b_{N_B} \leq 1$. The angle is stored in a bidimensional $m \times n$ matrix D with gray-scale component θ, with $0 \leq \theta < \pi$ (see Figure 3).

By summing every gray level in D, we obtain an histogram $H(x)$ that represent the angular distances between mesh M_A and M_B showed in Figure 4. On the X axis we represent the achievable angles between each pair of comparisons (sorted from 0° degree to 180° degree), while on the Y axis we represent the total number of differences found. This means that two similar faces will have an histogram $H(x)$ with very high values on little angles, while two distinct faces will have differences more distributed. At this point, a convolution with a Gaussian function $G(x)$ (see Figure 5) is used for weigh the angle differences between M_A and M_B:

$$H(x) \circ G(x) = \sum_{x=0}^{k} \left(h(x) \cdot \frac{1}{\sigma\sqrt{2\pi}} e^{-\frac{x^2}{2\sigma^2}} \right)$$

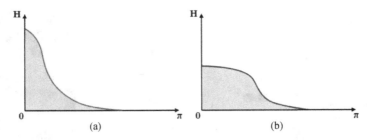

Figure 4. Example of histogram H to represent the angular distances. (a) shows a typical histogram between two similar Normal Maps, while (b) between two different Normal Maps.

In this matter, varying σ and k possible to change the sensibility of the recognition system.

3.6. *The Reference Database*

One of the aims in experiments conducted on the proposed method was to test its performance under controlled conditions, so we decided to build a face database based on surface mesh resulting from a feature guided warping of a standard face mesh. More precisely, every face model in the database has been created deforming a standard polygonal face mesh to closely fit a set of facial features extracted from front and side images of each individual to be enrolled in the system.

The standard face mesh used in the dataset has about 7K triangular facets, and even if it is certainly possible to use mesh with higher level of detail (LOD), we found this resolution to be adequate to the recognition purpose. This is mainly due to the optimized tessellation which privileges key area such as eyes, nose and lips whereas a typical mesh produced by 3D scanner features almost evenly spaced vertices.

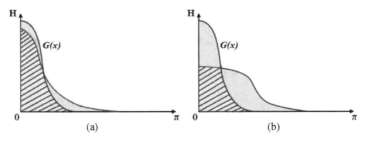

Figure 5. Convolution between Histogram H(x) and Gaussian function G(x).

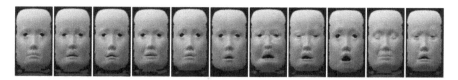

Figure 6. An example of normal maps of the same subject featuring different facial expression: neutral, rage (moderate), fear, smile (closed), doubt, surprise (moderate), rage (extreme), despise, surprise (extreme), closed eyes, disgust.

The full database includes 50 different individuals (30 males and 20 females, age ranging from 19 to 40) each featuring the following 10 different expressions: neutral, rage (moderate), fear, smile (closed), doubt, surprise (moderate), rage (extreme), despise, surprise (extreme), closed eyes, disgust (see Figure 6).

3.7. *Facial Expression Robustness*

To improve the robustness of the method to facial expressions we use a subject-specific pre-calculated map, called the expressive weighted mask.

This mask, which shares the same size of normal map and difference map, contains for each pixel an 8 bit weight encoding the local rigidity of the face surface based on the analysis of a pre-built set of nine facial expressions of the same subject in the database. Indeed, for each subject enrolled, a set of nine previously acquired expressive variations is compared to the neutral face resulting in nine difference maps. The average of this set of difference maps specific to the same individual represent its expressive weighted mask.

More precisely, given a generic face with its normal map N_0 (neutral face) and the set of normal maps N_1, N_2, … ,N_n (the expressive variations), we first calculate the set of difference map D_1, D_2, … ,D_n resulting from {'N_0 - N_1', 'N_0 − N_2', … , 'N_0 − N_n'} (see Figure 7-a). The average of set {D_1, D_2, … ,D_n} is the expressive weighted mask (see Figure 7-b).

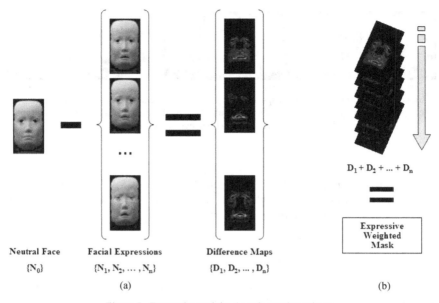

Neutral Face   Facial Expressions   Difference Maps
{N_0}   {$N_1, N_2, \dots, N_n$}   {$D_1, D_2, \dots, D_n$}

(a)   (b)

$D_1 + D_2 + \dots + D_n$

Expressive
Weighted
Mask

Figure 7. Expressive weighted mask creation scheme.

4. Experiment and Discussion

We present the results of our method on a 3D database of human faces, featuring different races, sex, ages, and expressions. We have evaluated the recognition rate performing a one-to-one comparison of a probe set of 3D models with a gallery set of 3D models with neutral expression. The recognition rate showed to be very good reaching 100% using semi-automatic alignment. The results are generally better than those obtained by many 2D algorithms but the lack of a standard 2D/3D reference face dataset make the comparison difficult. More specifically, in Table 1 are illustrated the results of precision/recall of recognition system.

5. Conclusions

We presented a method for tridimensional face recognition based on normal map, a 2D array storing information about local curvature of face surface, aimed to biometrical applications.

The method proved to be simple, robust to posing and expression variations, relatively fast and with an high average recognition rate. Experimental results show that wavelet compression of normal map could greatly reduce the size of face descriptor not significantly affecting the recognition precision.

As the normal map is a 2D mapping of mesh features, future research could well integrate additional 2D color info (texture) acquired during the same enrolment session. Implementing a true multi-modal version of the basic algorithm which correlates the texture and normal map could further enhance the discriminating power even for complex 3D recognition issues such as the presence of beard, moustache, eyeglasses, etc.

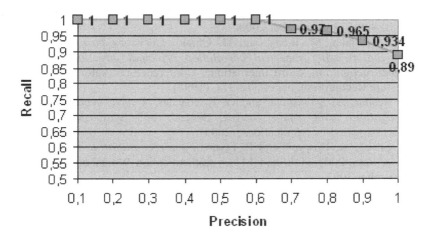

Table 1. Precision/Recall using normal map 128×128, Gaussian function G(x) (with σ = 4.5 and k = 50) and mask size 3.

References

1. C. Beumier, M. Acheroy, *Automatic Face Authentication from 3D surface*, British Machine Vision Conference (BVMC 98), 1998.
2. X. Gu, S. Gortler, H. Hoppe, *Geometry image*, ACM SIGGRAPH 2002, pages 355-361.
3. S. Ricciardi, G. Sabatino, *A Method For 3D Face Rrcognition Based On Mesh Normals*, Multimedia Databases And Image Communication (MDIC04).
4. K.W. Bowyer, K. Chang, P. A. Flynn, *Survey of 3D and Multi-Modal 3D+2D Face Recognition*, ICPR 2004.
5. J. Y. Cartoux, J. T. LaPreste, and M. Richetin, *Face authentication or recognition by profile extraction from range images*, Proceedings of the Workshop on Interpretation of 3D Scenes, pages 194-199, November 1989.

6. T. Nagamine, T. Uemura, and I. Masuda, *3D facial image analysis for human identification.* International Conference on Pattern Recognition (ICPR 1992), pages 324-327, (1992).
7. G. Gordon, *Face recognition based on depth and curvature features.* Computer Vision and Pattern Recognition (CVPR), pages 108-110, June 1992.
8. B. Achermann, X. Jiang, and H. Bunke, *Face recognition using range images.* International Conference on Virtual Systems and MultiMedia, pages 129-136, (1997).
9. B. Achermann and H. Bunke, *Classifying range images of human faces with Hausdorff distance*, 15-th International Conference on Pattern Recognition, pages 809-813, September 2000.
10. H. T. Tanaka, M. Ikeda, and H. Chiaki, *Curvature-based face surface recognition using spherical correlation principal directions for curved object recognition*, Third International Conference on Automated Face and Gesture Recognition, pages 372-377, (1998).
11. C. Hesher, A. Srivastava, and G. Erlebacher, *A novel technique for face recognition using range images*, Seventh Int'l Symposium on Signal Processing and Its Applications, (2003).
12. K. Chang, K. Bowyer, and P. Flynn, *Face recognition using 2D and 3D facial data*, 2003 Multimodal User Authentication Workshop, pages 25-32, December 2003.
13. G. Medioni and R. Waupotitsch, *Face recognition and modeling in 3D. IEEE International* Workshop on Analysis and Modeling of Faces and Gestures (AMFG 2003), pages 232-233, October 2003.
14. A. M. Bronstein, M. M. Bronstein, and R. Kimmel, *Expression-invariant 3D face recognition*, AudioandVideo-Based Person Authentication (AVBPA 2003), LCNS 2688, J. Kittler and M.S. Nixon, eds.:62-70, (2003).
15. C. Beumier and M. Acheroy, *Face verification from 3D and grey level cues*, Pattern Recognition Letters,22:1321-1329, 2001.
16. Y.Wang, C. Chua, and Y. Ho, *Facial feature detection and face recognition from 2D and 3D images*, Pattern Recognition Letters, 23:1191-1202, (2002).

ENTROPY MEASURES IN IMAGE CLASSIFICATION

ANDREA CASANOVA[*], VITO DI GESÙ[†], GIOSUÈ LO BOSCO[†],
SERGIO VITULANO[*]

[*]*Dipartimento di Scienze Mediche e Internistiche, Università di Cagliari
Policlinico Universitario, Monserrato, Cagliari*

[†]*Dipartimento di Matematica ed Applicazioni, Università di Palermo
Via Archirafi 34, 90123, Palermo*

The chapter introduces new entropy measures that use the image information content such as grey levels and their topological distribution in the image domain in order to perform the classification of the image itself. The main aim of the chapter is to study the role of the image entropy in perceptual tasks and to compare the proposed approach with others well-known methods. Experiments have been carried out on medical images (mammograms) due to their variability and complexity. The image entropy approach seems to work quite well and it is less time-consuming if compared with the other methods.

1. Introduction

The concept of entropy has been developed in thermodynamics in order to characterize the ability of a system in changing his status. Measures of system entropy are usually functions defined in the phase space and they reach the maximum or minimum value, depending on the contextual definition, whenever system variables are uniformly distributed.

This concept has been borrow in communication systems for coding purposes and data compression [1,2]. Entropy based functional have been also used in image and signal analysis to perform deconvolution [3] and segmentation [4], to measure the pictorial information [5], and to define image differences [6].

In the following, entropy measures, defined on the feature space, are introduced. In some cases they can be normalized in the interval [0,1] and are named. The idea of measure the entropy of an image for classification purposes is not a new one. For example, the idea of cross entropy was used to define the distance which is popularly known as Kullback-Leibler [7] information distance.

However, this distance between two distributions should not be considered as the true distance as it is not symmetric and does not satisfy the triangle inequality [8]. It may be mentioned that in early sixties connections between statistics, quantum mechanics and information theory have been thoroughly studied by several authors [9], using Shannon maximum entropy principle. Caianiello [10] proposed that such a connection can be obtained in the natural *meeting ground of geometry*. In the following we present two classes of entropic measures: the *fuzzy entropy* [11] and the *Vitulano's entropy* [12].

The choice to use mammograms id due to the development of new imaging methods for medical diagnosis that has significantly widened the scope of the images available to physicians[26,27].

Also because the inner difficulty in homogeneous databases – such as those utilized by application in a specific field – e.g. medicine – are characterized by having very small differences among the objects; the most effective approaches to data are based on object contour shapes and spatial relationships among them. Images in the databases present a much wider range of variability and therefore can usually be represented by coarser global features, such as texture or colour percentage.

The problem is to realize a mapping from the set of all possible images (image space) to the set – usually smaller – of all possible features value (feature space).

The most relevant points related to the problem is the qualitative and quantitative choice of these features.

The analysis and the classification of mammographies are problems not yet resolved. In order to classify this kind of signal is necessary to distinguish, with a high reliability, between benignant or malignant masses, benignant or malignant microcalcification (see Figure 1).

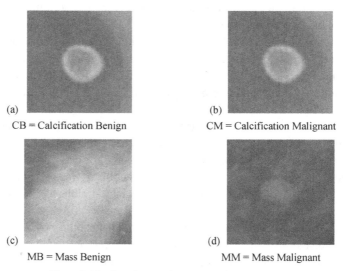

(a)	(b)
CB = Calcification Benign	CM = Calcification Malignant
(c)	(d)
MB = Mass Benign	MM = Mass Malignant

Figure 1. The four classes of breast mammography classes.

The early detection of small, non palpable breast cancers is the aim of CAD (Computer-Aided Diagnosis). An early sign of disease in 30-50% of mammographically detected cases is the appearance of clusters of fine, granular microcalcifications whose individual grains typically range in size from 0.05-1 mm in diameter [12]. Individual microcalcifications are difficult to detect because of variations in their shape and size because they are embedded in and camouflaged by varying densities of parenchymal tissue structures [13]. Indeed, recent estimates indicate that between 10% and 30% of breast lesions (of all types) are missed by radiologist during routine screening. CAD schemes using digital image processing techniques have the goal of improving the detection performance and throughput of screening mammography. Typically, CAD systems are designed to provide a "second opinion", to aid rather than replace the radiologist.

In the chapter we use the DDSM [14], where there are 12 or 16 bits images and with the cluster: 695 normal cases; 914 cancer cases and 677 benign cases. Each case is composed of four different mammograms.

Section 2 provides a review of recent methods. Section 3 is dedicated to the description of the entropy measures and their properties. Section 4 shows the results obtained from the experimentation. Final remarks are given in Section 5.

2. Related Works

An important branch of CAD methods in mammography employs wavelet transforms for feature enhancement [15, 16]. The general approach is:
- compute the forward wavelet transform of the image;
- nonlinearly transform or adaptively weight the wavelet coefficients;
- compute the inverse transform.

Richardson [17] showed that the details components of the lowest octaves (i.e. those containing the finest structure) can be useful in enhancing the visibility of microcalcification. Laine [18] achieves a scale-dependent enhancement of mammograms by selectively weighting and scaling the details computed using a first derivative of a Gaussian wavelet. In later work a dyadic wavelet transform method is shown to be equivalent to unsharp masking at multiple scales. Barman [19,23,24,25] employs a hybrid of wavelet and feature extraction techniques for micorcalcifications detection. The outputs from multiple scale quadrature filters are processed by specialized object extraction algorithms, employing size, orientation, relative brightness and shape feature. Clusters of microcalcifications are tagged by examining and detecting likely combinations of features in the object list. Qian [15] enhances microcalcifications by cascading adaptive spatial filtering with multi resolution decomposition and reconstruction. Yoshida [16] improves the visibility of microcalcification by reconstructing mammograms from selected sub bands. Post-detection using morphological operators and thresholding achieves a sensibility of 85% true clusters detected at five false positive clusters per image when tested on a 100μ resolution database of 39 mammograms. Strickland [13] show the application of wavelets in mammography employing a wavelet transform with acts as a bank of multiscale matched filters for detecting microcalcifications. The sub band images create by a four-octave wavelet decomposition are thresholded and combined to yield a map of detected pixels. Segmentation of microcalcifications is realised by weighting the sub-bands of the detected sites before computing the inverse wavelet transform.

Our contribution to the analysis and CAD methods is to introduce an entropy measure of the signal in order to cluster mass and microcalcification in mammograms.

The Vitulano's entropy method acts in the following way:

1.   a certain number of disjoint sub-regions are chosen in the region under acts in the mammograms. In this chapter we utilize nine sub regions;
2.   whit a linear method *spiral* [20] we transform the two dimensional signal contained in the sub region in a one-dimensional signal (see Figure 2);
3.   on each 1-D signal we compute the entropy features;
4.   only for those signal with a non significative measures of the entropy features we apply the HER method [21,22].

The general structure of the Fuzzy-entropy method can be sketched in the following way:

1.   compute a measure of fuzzy-entropy that is function of the distribution of the pixel grey levels, as it will be described below. The entropy measure characterizes the differences between the mean intensity value and the set of the minimum intensity values distribution;
2.   apply a Bayesian classifier in the new feature space that assign to each image a measure of fuzzy-entropy.

3. Proposed Methods

In the following two measure of entropies are introduced and their properties outlined.

3.1. *Fuzzy Entropies*

In the following we introduce four types of fuzzy entropies. They are said "fuzzy" because they satisfy some of the formal properties of the classical entropy introduced by Shannon; however, they are computed on image features that are not probabilities.

The input image, $f \equiv (f_1, \ldots, f_n)$, is represented as a linear signal after the transformation from raster to spiral indexing.

Moreover, we define the vector $h \equiv (h_1, \ldots, h_n)$, with:

$$h_i = \begin{cases} m - f_i & m > f_i \\ 0 & otherwise \end{cases} \quad with \ m = mean(f) \ for \ i = 1, \ldots n$$

That represents all values that are below the mean value, m.

Starting from these definitions we define the following measure of fuzzy entropies:

1) $G_0 = \dfrac{1}{\log 2} \times \left(-\eta \times \log(\eta) - (1 - \eta) \times \log(1 - \eta) \right)$

2) $G_1 = \dfrac{2\sqrt{e}}{e - 1} \times \left(\eta \times e^{1-\eta} - \eta \times e^{\eta-1} \right)$

3) $G_2 = 4 \times \eta \times (1 - \eta)$

4) $G_3 = -\dfrac{1}{\log n} \sum_{i=1}^{n} h_i \times \log h_i$

with $\eta = \dfrac{1}{n} \sum_{i=1}^{n} |h_i|$ or $\eta = \sqrt{\dfrac{1}{n} \sum_{i=1}^{n} h_i^2}$.

Note that η measure the distance between the constant function $f = m$ and the function h. Moreover, all these measures of entropy are convex and their values range in the interval [0,1]. The maximum of Gj (for $i = 0,1,2$) is equal to 1 and is reached for $\eta = 1/2$ while the maximum of G_3 is reached for $h_i = 1/n$ and is also equal to 1. More details about the fuzzy entropies here introduced can be found in Caianiello[10].

3.2. *Vitulano's Entropy Measures*

Let us introduce some definition before presenting the main steps of the method proposed in this work:

Definition 1: we define "signal crest" the part of the signal contained between the absolute minimum and the absolute maximum of the signal itself;

Definition 2: we define "signal entropy" the ratio between the crest energy and the signal energy, expressed as follow:

$$S = \frac{\sum\limits_{t=1}^{D}(y_t - y_m)}{\sum\limits_{t=1}^{D} y_t} \tag{1}$$

where:

D=signal domain;
y_t=amplitude of the signal at the-t^h point;
y_m=amplitude of the signal at the absolute minimum;

The entropy S can assume one of the values contained in the [0,1] interval.
The 0 value occurs when the absolute minimum and the absolute maximum of the signal have the same value (i.e. flat signal); instead the 1 value occurs when the signal is monotone increasing (i.e. triangular signal).
The Equation (1) can be written in a more simple way; in fact if we define:

$$h' = \frac{\sum\limits_{t=1}^{D}(y_t - y_m)}{D} \quad \text{and} \quad h = \frac{\sum\limits_{t=1}^{D} y_t}{D} \tag{2}$$

We can write Equation (1) as:

$$S = \frac{h'}{h} \tag{3}$$

The Equation (3) shows that the entropy is due to the ratio between h' and h, that, roughly speaking, may be considered as a measure of the signal "roughness" with respect to the signal energy.

In a previous work we have introduced a linear transformation, "spiral", of 2D signal in a 1D one; with this transformation any picture, or a part of it, may be transformed in a 1D signal without loss of information.

The main steps of the proposed method are the following:

1. We select the region of interest r_i from each of the pictures belonging to the data set;
2. We perform the transformation of the 2D signal of the region r_i in a 1D signal via the application of the spiral linear transformation;
3. We compute the entropy value S for each of the signal y_i.

The days where computers were text-only systems are long gone. Nowadays, even low-end personal computers are able to display, employ and process images – at least in the form of icon- but usually in much more complex ways.

The typical user has several image files in his disk device; the high-end user or the graphic specialist may have thousands.

Furthermore, there are computer systems that are entirely devoted to the archival or treatments of image: many multimedia databases are made in great part by images, and several applications in a wide range of specific fields rely on digital images for many of their functions (i.e. PACS system in medicine).

As the number of images available to a system increases, the need for an automatic image retrieval system of some kind becomes more stringent. We believe that, for a first screening, the entropy of the signal query may be used with the purpose to select signal in a homogeneous data set.

Given the signal y_i as a query signal, we use its entropy value as a similarity measure between y_i and all the signals belonging to the data set.

In this way we realize a very strong reduction of the data set dimension; in fact we need only to store the entropy value of each of the signals instead of managing the whole picture data set or the 1D corresponding signals.

In order to verify the entropy method when applied to real signals, in this work we utilized breast mammographies as data set in which benignant or malignant masses are also included.

Our choice was due to the characteristics of these images, and to their high-degree of difficulties also for a human expert.

For each of the mammographies belonging to the DDSM database, the zone of suspected mass is given.

In each one of the suspected zone in the mammography we consider 9 disjoint regions of 25 x 25 pixels. Two examples of mammographies for a *MM* and *BM* classes are shown in Figures 3(a,b) respectively.

In Figure 2, the crest of the signals, obtained when the spiral transformation is applied respectively to the picture of Figures 1(d,c) is shown. This linearization shows the role and the significance of the signal entropy.

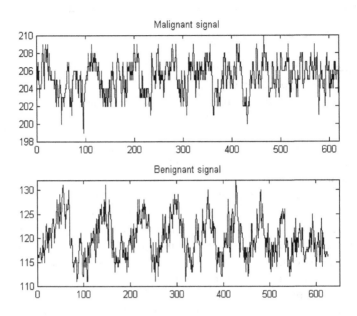

Figure 2. Crest of the MM (top) and BM (bottom) signal shown respectively in Figure 1(d,c) obtained after the application of spiral transformation.

In another previous work we have introduced HER, a method for the analysis and classification of 1D signals; HER was widely experimented on different signals (textures, contours, medical images and aerophotogrammetries).

The main features of HER are:

1. to weight, in a hierarchical way, each maximum in relation to its role with respect to the behaviour of the signal;
2. to order the extracted maximum in function of the extraction order, the distance of each maximum respect to the previous one;
3. to classify each signal in function of the number of maximum extracted, amount of the energy used for the extraction, value (σ) of the energy to each of the maximum associated.

4. Experimental Results

The role of entropy-measures in analysis and classification problems has been evaluated on real images representing mammographies. Images have been provided by site http://marathon.csee.usf.edu/Mammography/Database.html. Results show that an improvement can be achieved considering both fuzzy and Vitulano measures.

4.1. *Experiments with Fuzzy Entropies*

Figures 3a,b,c,d show the distribution of the four entropy measures for the classes *MB*, *MM*. Table 1 shows the mean values, μ, and the standard deviation, σ, of the distributions of G_0, G_1, G_2, G_3 and for the two classes. The result indicates that in the average the entropy of classes *MM* is greater than the entropy of class *MB*. The four measures have been used as a new features space, allowing a better discrimination among these classes of diseases.

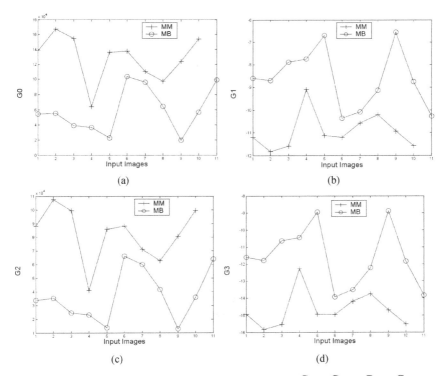

Figure 3. Entropy distributions for the *MM*, *MB* classes: a) G_0, b) G_{11}, c) G_2, d) G_3.

Table 1

	μ_{MM}	σ_{MM}	μ_{MB}	σ_{MB}
G_0	3.25	0.79	1.48	0.78
G_1	12.47	0.91	9.20	3.00
G_2	2.00	0.55	0.94	0.45
G_3	15.00	1.10	11.70	1.70

4.2. *Experiments with Vitulano's Entropy*

In this essay, we plan to propose entropy as a measurement of benignancy and malignancy of the case under examination.

The crucial point of the mentioned method, something common to many other proposed methods in the literature, is to determine the threshold value. The threshold value is been used by us to classify the case under examination, which means to assign it to the benignant class or to the malignant one. Of course, every time that real cases are being used, the sets of the elements, that we wish to select, are not disjointed.

The whole problem can be expressed in the following way: minimize the intersection of the sets instead of the union of the sets.

In this chapter, we have used a database that suggests, for every class contained in it, a training set.

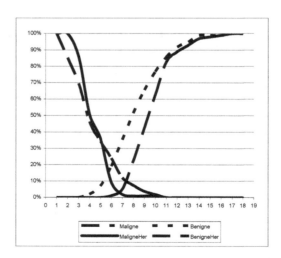

Figure 4. State of the obtained result, using the entropy method and HER.

In the graphic in Figure 4 we give the state of the obtained results, using the entropy method and HER to the training set regarding the malignant and benignant masses.

The curve concerning the malignant masses has been produced by making graphics, in percentages, of the cases that show a value of entropy bigger than the one of the interval under examination (i.e. 100% of the examined cases have values of entropy bigger than 1 and 0% of the cases have entropy bigger than 11).

The curve concerning the benignant masses shows how many cases, in percentage, have values of entropy less than the one regarding the interval under examination (i.e. in none of the cases exist value of entropy less than 2, in the interval of entropy 2-16 are embraced 100% of the benignant cases).

The value of the threshold is given by the abscissa of the common point between the two curves (the value that maximizes the number of the cases in support of the malignant and minimizes the number of the cases against to the benignant ones).

The cases contained in the intersection set between the set of cases with malignant masses and the set of cases with benignant masses, require a greater attention and more accurate analysis, or completely different (i.e. biopsy).

Table 2: Results due to the crest method when applied to micro calcification.

Method	Malignant		Benignant	
	# Errors	Percentage	# Errors	Percentage
Fourier	70	51%	62	51%
Vitulano's Entropy	10	93%	9	93%
HER	6	96%	5	96%
Fuzzy Entropy	22	85%	6	95%

Table 3: Results due to the crest method when applied to mass.

Method	Malignant		Benignant	
	# Errors	Percentage	# Errors	Percentage
Fourier	51	53%	52	53%
Vitulano's Entropy	22	80%	20	80%
HER	5	95%	5	95%
Fuzzy Entropy	9	90%	18	82%

To study those cases, we applied the method HER with a further research. On Table 2, it is shown the obtained results. It is also given the results obtained by applying a high pass filter with a cut frequency which lets by 200 highest frequencies of Fourier spectrum.

Because of the strong interest in the detection of micro calcifications in mammographies, we decided to test the crest method also to this kind of signals, whose results are summarized on Table 3.

The analysis of the signals of the micro calcifications (Figure 5) highlights that for the malignant cases, the impulses are characterized by a small amount of energy (impulse area), a significant shape and a remarkable value of the entropy in the bottom of the signal if compared to the signals of the benignant ones.

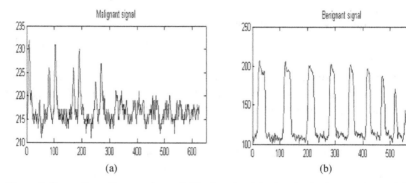

(a)   (b)

Figure 5. Crest of a malignant micro calcification signal (top) and a benignant micro calcification signal (bottom) after the application of spiral method.

5. Discussion and Final Remarks

The experimental results show the role of the entropy in perception. In particular, the use of the Fourier transforms and high pass filers do not show good performance unless of ad hoc tuning of given parameters. In fact, the shape, the power spectra or the approximation degree of the polynomial are not characterizing due to the nature of the signal.

Instead, the degree of disorder (entropy) of the image is in our case an important indicator; in fact, also the physician utilizes the texture disorder (parenchymal tissue structures) in the suspicious region of the image for the diagnosis of malignant or benignant.

The methods proposed in this work gets the guide reasons by observing that, when a malignant lesion comes up, not only it causes alterations in the cellular tissue, but also a greater disorder.

In other words, we feel that the alterations concerning the same tissue, can be a valid measure or an increasing of the malignancy of the lesion.

In Figure 5 we show the signal concerning two different tissues: a tissue hit by a malignant micro calcification and a tissue hit by a benignant micro calcification.

The comparison between the two signals reveals that, malignant micro calcification produces a bigger alteration (entropy) if compared to those one produced by benignant micro calcification.

It is remarkable that the entropy measures of the signal do not require a large amount of operations, therefore it is less computational time consuming.

References

1. F. Kossentini, M.J.T. Smith, C.F. Barnes, "Image coding using entropy-constrained residual vector quantization", in *IEEE Transactions on Image Processing* , **4** , pp.1349-1357, (1995).
2. Z. Xiong, K. Ramchandran, and M. T. Orchard, "Space-frequency quantization for wavelet image coding", in *IEEE Transactions on Image Processing*, **6**, N.5, pp. 677-693, (1997).
3. J. Skilling, R.K. Bryan, "Maximum entropy image reconstruction: general algorithm", *Month. Notices Roy. Astronom. Soc* , **211**, pp. 111-124, (1984).
4. C. Di Ruberto, M. Nappi and S. Vitulano "Different Methods to Segment Biomedical Images", *Pattern Recognition Letters,* **18**, nos. 11/13, pp. 1125-1131,(1998).
5. J. Zachar , S.S. Iyengar, "Informaton theoretic similarity measures for content based image retrieval", *Journal of the American Society for Information Science and Technology*, **52**, N.10, pp. 856-857, (2001).
6. V.Di Gesù, S.Roy, "Fuzzy measures for image distance", *in proc of Advances in Fuzzy Systems and Intelligent Technoligies* , F.Masulli, R.Parenti, G.Pasi Ed.s, Shaker Publishing , pp.156 -164, (2000).
7. S.C. Kullback, "Information Theory and Statisitcs", New York, N.Y., (1959).
8. T.M. Covar and J.A. Thomas, "Elements of Information Theory", John Wiley and Sons, INC., (1991).
9. E.T.Jaynes, "Information Theory and Statistical Mechanics", *Phys. Rev.,* **106**, pp. 620–630 (1957).
10. E.R.Caianiello, "Geometrical identification of quantum and information theories", *Lett. Nuovo Cimento*, **38**, pp. 539-543, (1983).
11. V. Di Gesù, S. Roy, "Pictorial indexes and soft image distances", in *Lecture Notes in Computer Science*, N.R.Pal and M. Sugeno Eds., pp. 200-215 (2002).

12. A.Casanova, V.Savona and S.Vitulano, "Entropy As A Feature In The Analysis And Classification Of Signals", *MDIC*, (2004).
13. I.W. Bassel, "Mammographic analysis of calcification", in *Radiol. Clin.No.Amer.* , **30**, pp. 93-105, (1992)
14. R.N. Strickland, H.Hahn, "Wavelet Transforms for detecting microcalcifications in Mammograms", *IEEE Trans. on Medical imaging*, **15**, *No.2*, (1996).
15. M. Heath, K.W. Bowyer, D. Kopans et al,. "Current status of the digital Database for Screening Mammography", *Digital Mammography* ,pp 457-460 Kluwer Academic Pub. (1998).
16. L. P. Clarke, "Tree structured non linear filter and wavelet transform for microcalcification segmentation in mammography", *Cancer Lett.*, **77**(2-3), pp. 173-181, (1994).
17. H. Yoshida, K. Doi and R. M. Nishikawa, "Application of The Wavelet Transform To Automated Detection of Clustered Microclacifications", *Digital Mammogram.*, Academic Reports of Tokyo Institute of Polytechnics, **16**, pp.24-37, (1994).
18. W.Richardson, "Non linear filtering and multiscale texture discrimination for mammograms", in *Mathematical Methods Med. Imag., Proc. SPIE 1768*, pp. 293-305, (1992).
19. A. Laine, S. Song, "Multiscale wavelet representation for mammography feature analysis", in *Mathematical Methods Med. Imag., Proc. SPIE 1768*, pp. 23-25, (1992)
20. H. Bårman, G. H. Granlund, "Using simple local Fourier domain models for computer-aided analysis of mammograms", *Proc. 8th Scandinavian Conf. Image Anal.*, pp. 479-486 (1993).
21. R. Distasi, S. Vitulano, "A hierarchical representation for content-based image retrieval", *Jour. Of Visual Lang. and Comp.*, **5**, pp. 369-382, (2000).
22. R. Distasi, M. Nappi, S. Vitulano, et al., "HEAT: Hierarchical Entropy Approach for Texture Indexing in Image Databases", *Jour. Of Soft. Eng. And Knowl.*, **12**(5), pp. 501-522, (2002).
23. C. Brambilla, A. Della Ventura, I. Gagliardi, R. Schettini, "Multiresolution wavelet transform and supervised learning for content-based image retrieval", *IEEE Int. Conf. on Multimedia Computing and System*, **1**, pp.183-188, (1999).
24. E.G. M. Petrakis, C. Faloutsos, "Similarity searching in medical image databases", *IEEE Trans. Knowledge and Data Eng.*, **9**(3), pp. 435-447, (1997).
25. R. Brunelli, O. Mich, "Image retrieval by examples", *IEEE Trans. On Multimedia*, **2**(3), pp. 164-171, (2000).

26. M. Heath, K. Chang, K. Bowyer, D. Kopans et al, "Current status of digital database for screening mammography", *Digital Mammography*, Kluwer Academic Pub., pp. 457-460, (1998).
27. M. Melloul, L. Joskowicz, "Segmentation of microcalcification in X-ray mammograms using entropy thresholding", *CARS 2002*, H.U.Lemke et al. Editors, (2002).

COMPLEX OBJECTS CLASSIFIED BY MORPHOLOGICAL SHAPE ANALYSIS AND ELLIPTICAL FOURIER DESCRIPTORS

B. BALLARÒ, D. TEGOLO, C. VALENTI

Dipartimento di Matematica e Applicazioni,
Università degli Studi di Palermo, Italy
E-mail: ballaro,tegolo,cvalenti@math.unipa.it

C. TRIPODO

Istituto di Anatomia Patologica,
Università degli Studi di Palermo, Italy
E-mail: tripodo@unipa.it

This chapter deals with the classification of complex objects by morphological shape analysis and elliptical Fourier descriptors. An unsupervised method has been proposed to identify components with specific shapes by a simple edge detector and to classify them via the description of their contours. A particular application has been arranged in order to evaluate the goodness of this approach when discriminating between normal and pathological human megakaryocytes. Alterations in these cells can occur in many pathological processes and in such cases the pattern, size and shape of the cytoplasm and/or of the nucleus are extremely varied.

1. Introduction

Machine perception is one of the most significant challenge in the research field of artificial vision. Expertise, skill, vision, and consciousness to problem are some of the characteristics for human to recognize and to classify at the best a scene with complex objects. A complex object can be defined as something not easy to classify for naive human. This simple definition can be formalized in term of features: let define a complex object as an element in which a large number of features are needed to classify it with an error factor.

The proposed methodology is based on a few number of features (elliptical Fourier descriptors) and a small number of images are devoted to training. The method has been tested in the medicine field, to discriminate between normal and pathological human megakaryocytes. Section 2 describes the mock-up of the input images; the object representation is introduced in section 3; experimental results and conclusions are given in section 4.

2. Preprocessing and Segmentation

Mathematical morphology is a branch of digital image analysis which uses concepts of algebra and geometry [1]. Its theoretical foundations have been well established and here we will just recall the standard terminology and a few notations.

Given an image I with grey levels in $[0,255]$ and the flat structuring element D_r obtained as the approximated discrete disk of radius r, let us define the erosion ε and the dilation δ:

$$\varepsilon_r(I)(\underline{p}) = \min_{\underline{q} \in D_r} I(\underline{p} + \underline{q}) \quad \text{and} \quad \delta_r(I)(\underline{p}) = \min_{\underline{q} \in D_r} I(\underline{p} + \underline{q}).$$

Both erosion and dilation in general are not invertible, but we can define two morphological operators, called opening γ and closing φ, which should recover as much as possible the original image I:

$$\gamma_r(I) = \delta_r(\varepsilon_r(I)) \quad \text{and} \quad \varphi_r(I) = \varepsilon_r(\delta_r(I)).$$

The usual application of the opening is the removing of small objects from I while preserving the shape and size of larger objects. Viceversa the closing fills in the smaller gaps in I. The opening and closing can be combined to build the top-hat th and bottom-hat bh operators:

$$th_r(I) = \max\{0, I - \gamma_r(I)\} \quad \text{and} \quad bh_r(I) = \max\{0, \varphi_r(I) - I\}$$

which let enhance the contrast of I by using the following formula:

$$ec_r(I) = \max\{0, \min\{255, I + th_r(I)\} - bh_r(I)\}.$$

The edge detector can be sketched by the following sequence of main operations (see also Figure 1):

a. enhance the contrast of the dilated grey level photomicrograph: $I' \leftarrow ec_1(\delta_1(I))$;
b. create the mask I_c for the cytoplasm by thresholding the bigger bright areas: $I_c \leftarrow \{I' : I' \leq \tau_c\}$; $I_c \leftarrow \{I_c : |I_c| \geq 3000\}$;
c. create the mask I_n for the nucleus by thresholding the dark areas within I_c: $I_n \leftarrow \{I' : I' \leq \tau_n\} \cap I_c$; $I_n \leftarrow \{I_n : |I_n| \geq 100\}$;
d. smooth the contour of the cytoplasm: $I_c \leftarrow \{I_c : I_n \leq I_c\}$; $I_c \leftarrow \varphi_4(\gamma_4(I_c))$;
e. locate the cell close to the centre of the photo: $I_c \leftarrow \{I_c : \min\|I_c - \text{size}(I)/2\|\}$;
f. eliminate spurs in the nucleus and fill its smallest holes: $I_n \leftarrow \varphi_2(I_n)$.

All radii of the structuring elements have been chosen according to the size of the input images. The thresholding values τ_c and τ_n can be effectively determined by using a k-nearest neighbour on the luminance histogram. In this case, the starting seeds for the cytoplasm and the nucleus sets have been experimentally determined. Lastly, it must be noted that I_n is computed just to enhance I_c, but we believe that it can be used to extract further features of the cells.

3. Elliptical Fourier Descriptors

The main goal of the elliptical Fourier analysis is to approximate a closed contour as the sum of elliptical harmonics. Kuhl and Giardina use four Fourier coefficients a_n, b_n, c_n and d_n for each harmonic, and to identify the closed contour of k points they consider N harmonics [2]:

$$a_n = \frac{T}{2\pi^2 n^2} \sum_{i=1}^{k} \frac{dx_i}{dt_i} \left(\cos\frac{2\pi n t_i}{T} - \cos\frac{2\pi n t_{i-1}}{T} \right),$$

$$b_n = \frac{T}{2\pi^2 n^2} \sum_{i=1}^{k} \frac{dx_i}{dt_i} \left(\sin\frac{2\pi n t_i}{T} - \sin\frac{2\pi n t_{i-1}}{T} \right),$$

$$c_n = \frac{T}{2\pi^2 n^2} \sum_{i=1}^{k} \frac{dy_i}{dt_i} \left(\cos\frac{2\pi n t_i}{T} - \cos\frac{2\pi n t_{i-1}}{T} \right),$$

$$d_n = \frac{T}{2\pi^2 n^2} \sum_{i=1}^{k} \frac{dy_i}{dt_i} \left(\sin\frac{2\pi n t_i}{T} - \sin\frac{2\pi n t_{i-1}}{T} \right).$$

From a geometrical point of view a_i and b_i (c_i and d_i) represent the projection on the x (y) axes of the semimajor and of the semiminor axis of the ith harmonic.

The inverse process recovers the ith pixel of the contour from the harmonics:

$$X_i = X_c + \sum_{n=1}^{N} \left(a_n \cos\frac{2\pi n t_i}{T} + b_n \sin\frac{2\pi n t_i}{T} \right),$$

$$Y_i = Y_c + \sum_{n=1}^{N} \left(c_n \cos\frac{2\pi n t_i}{T} + d_n \sin\frac{2\pi n t_i}{T} \right)$$

where X_c and Y_c are the coordinates of the centroid of the region delimited by the contour:

$$X_c = \frac{1}{T}\sum_{i=1}^{k}\left(\frac{dx_i}{2dt_i}\left(t_i^2 - t_{i-1}^2\right) + \left(\sum_{j=1}^{i-1}dx_j - \frac{dx_i}{dt_i}\sum_{j=1}^{i-1}dt_j\right)\left(t_i - t_{i-1}\right)\right),$$

$$Y_c = \frac{1}{T}\sum_{i=1}^{k}\left(\frac{dy_i}{2dt_i}\left(t_i^2 - t_{i-1}^2\right) + \left(\sum_{j=1}^{i-1}dy_j - \frac{dy_i}{dt_i}\sum_{j=1}^{i-1}dt_j\right)\left(t_i - t_{i-1}\right)\right).$$

4. Results and Remarks

The experiment was conducted on high power magnification (400×) photomicrographs (577×763 pixels), taken from haematoxylin-and-eosin stained 3μ thick sections of formalin-fixed, paraffin embedded bone marrow trephine biopsies, from patients with Philadelpia-negative Chronic Myeloproliferative Disorders (CMPDs) and with reactive thormbocytosys. The morphology of the megakaryocytes (MKCs) was normal or well-preserved in reactive conditions, in which the MKCs showed round-to-oval shape, normal size of the cytoplasm and multi-lobulated nucleus. In cases of CMPDs the MKCs appeared often enlarged in size, with over-abundant cytoplasm, irregular shape, and hypo- or hyper-lobulated nucleus.

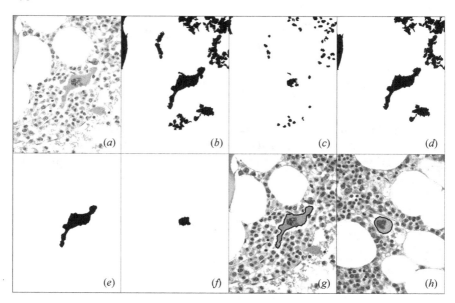

Figure 1. The edge detector applied on a pathological megakaryocyte (a-f). All naked nuclei have been correctly eliminated. The final contour of the cytoplasm has been superimposed on the input image (g), which shows a more abundant and irregular cytoplasm compared to a normal one (h).

In order to validate the correctness of the new classifier, based on the *k*-nearest neighbour method, we compared its output with the photo-interpretation provided by the pathologists. The new technique lets distinguish between pathological and normal cells with a recognition rate of 90% and 81% respectively, by using a bootstrap approach. The results so far obtained are encouraging though they have highlighted that more features (solidity, fractal dimension and eccentricity of the megakaryocytes, ...) should be considered to improve the efficiency of the classifier [3]. Multiple alterations (nucleus with multiple lobulations, coarse-grained nuclear chromatin, ...) can occur in many pathological processes that involve megakaryopoiesis. In such cases, the size and shape of the cytoplasm and/or of the nucleus and the chromatin pattern can be extremely varied [4].

Previous works on the automatic analysis of cells required a handmade segmentation. Although all threshold values have been predetermined or can be automatically computed, that is, the whole algorithm is unsupervised, we want to stress that our method should be considered as a fast preprocessing tool to help experts during the diagnosis phase. Moreover, it must be noted that the features and the methodologies here introduced are general and can be extended to solve different object recognition problems.

References

1. P. Soille, *Morphological Image Analysis*, Springer-Verlag, Second Edition (2003).
2. F.P. Kuhl and C.R. Giardina, *Elliptic Fourier Feature of a Closed Contour*, Computer Graphics and Image Processing, **18**, 236–258 (1982).
3. M. Beksaç, M.S. Beksaç, V.B. Tipi, H.A. Duru, M.U. Karakaş and A.N. Çakar, *An Artificial Intelligent Diagnostic System on Differential Recognition of Hematopoietic Cells From Microscopic Images*, Cytometry (Communications in Clinical Cytometry), **30**, 145–150 (1997).
4. J. Thiele, H.M. Kvasnicka and R. Fischer, *Histochemistry and morphometry on bone marrow biopsies in chronic myeloproliferative disorders - aids to diagnosis and classification*, Ann. Hematol., **78**, 11, 495–506 (1999).

VISUAL ATTENTION MECHANISMS FOR INFORMATION VISUALIZATION

ROBERTO MARMO

Dipartimento Informatica, Università di Pavia, via Ferrata 1, 27100 Pavia, Italy
email: marmo@vision.unipv.it

MARIO VALLE

Visualization Group, Swiss National Supercomputing Centre (CSCS)
Via Cantonale Galleria 2, 6928 Manno, Switzerland, email: mvalle@cscs.ch

Due to the overwhelming amount of information contained in the images produced by an information visualization tool, an important requirement for any visualization technique is that they should support rapid, accurate, and effortless visual exploration. We address this goal converting information into a graphical representation that takes better advantage of the human visual attention mechanisms.

1. Information Visualization

In 1983, Edward Tufte [32] noted "often the most effective way to describe, explore, and summarize a set of numbers, even a very large set, is to look at pictures of those numbers". Information visualization provides techniques for transforming data and information that are not inherently spatial into a visual form, facilitating their understanding [4,5].

Unfortunately, often there are nice visualizations that do not help understanding and do not create insight, because they ignore the human visual perception rules and are so complex that all the attention is wasted in understanding the image and not in extracting information from the data.

We approach information visualization by defining a set of requirements for each visualization technique:

1. shared data: the technique should be able to display independent data values simultaneously;
2. speed: users should be able to obtain information about any of the data values quickly;
3. accuracy: information should accurately represent structures and relationship between data values.

2. Visual Attention Mechanisms

The processing capabilities of the visual system are resource-limited and it is not conceivable to deal in exhaustive mode with the huge amount of visual information contained in a typical visualization image. Realistic performances can be only achieved applying attentional mechanisms, to allow the acquisition of more information in a single glance [3].

An attentional mechanism selects only the information from a given spatial location to act in the higher perceptual stages [28, 30]. Early visual information processing is thus characterized by two functionally distinct modes: pre-attentive and attentive.

In the pre-attentive mode, the information is processed in a spatially parallel manner in order to detect regions of potential interest within its field of view. The execution is characterized by a complete independence from the number of elements, an almost instantaneous execution, the lack of sophisticated scrutiny, a large visual field. The particular question investigated is whether rapid and accurate estimation is possible using these preattentive features. Tasks that can be performed in less than 250 milliseconds are considered pre-attentive, because within this period the human visual system cannot decide to change its focus of attention. Therefore, pre-attentive tasks require only a single glance at the displayed image.

In the attentive mode, the allocation of attentional resources to specific locations or objects is needed for more complex analysis. A small aperture of focal attention scrutinizes a sequence of regions of interest. The object can be consciously identified only in this attentional aperture.

The phenomenon of detection in the scene of targets characterized by a single feature not shared by other elements (usually called distractors), is called pop-out. In this case, the subject sees only a blur until suddenly the target jumps out right in front of him.

A tentative list of features, and related references, that pop-out during visual search is [11, 12]:
1.   3D depth cues [10];
2.   3D orientation [9, 10, 22];
3.   artistic properties [16, 17, 18];
4.   binocular lustre [34];
5.   closure [8, 31];
6.   color (hue) [1, 2, 7, 13, 15, 21, 23, 24];
7.   curvature [31];
8.   direction of motion [6, 25];
9.   flicker: [20];
10. intensity: [3, 31];
11. intersection [20];
12. length [31];
13. lighting direction [9];

14. line blob orientation [20, 26, 33, 35];
15. number [11, 20, 27];
16. size [29];
17. stereoscopic depth [25];
18. terminators [20];
19. texture properties [14, 15, 19];
20. width [27].

Using those features to represent properties within and relationships among data elements make possible a preattentive acquisition and understanding of the information contained in the visualized dataset.

A simple example of a pre-attentive task is the detection of a white circle (target) in a group of black circles as shown in Figure 1.

A viewer can tell at a glance whether the target is present or absent. A unique feature is used by the low-level visual system to rapidly identify the presence or absence of the target. Unfortunately, an intuitive combination of different features can lead to visual interference. A conjunction target item is made up of two or more features, only one of which is contained in each of the distractors. Figure 2 shows an example of conjunction search.

The target (white circle) contains two features: white and circular. One of these features is present in each of the distractor objects (white squares and black circles). Studies show that the target cannot be pre-attentively detected, forcing viewers to search serially through the image to find it.

This mechanism justifies the aphorism 'Presence is Parallel, Absence is Serial'. While there is a pooled response for the presence of a feature not shared by distractors, a target is pre-attentively invisible if it is defined only by the *absence* of a feature that is present in all the distractors. If we measure the pooled response to the relevant feature, we can expect to see a difference between scenes containing N-1 instances and scenes containing N instances of the target. Soon the difference becomes unreliable due to system noise, and subjects are forced to search the scene serially.

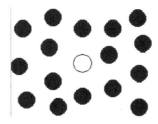

Figure 1. Example of pre-attentive task: detection of a white circle.

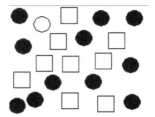

Figure 2. Example of pre-attentive task: detection conjunction target.

Figure 3 shows an example of this effect: the left region contains several circles, one of them with a crossing vertical segment; the right region vice versa contains just one plain circle, all the others have the crossing segment. The odd item is quite evident on the left. Instead, on the right a serial scrutiny is required.

Figure 4 shows three cases of regions composed by two different textures. In the leftmost region, the left segment is composed by the letter L, the one on the right by the letter T. The middle region contains letters L and T randomly distributed, but the left segment they are grey and on the right black. The rightmost region contains L and T letters randomly distributed and both letters can be black or grey: on the left segment T, letters are black and L letters are brighter, on the right segment vice versa. The partition into two texture sections is evident in the left and middle regions and not detectable in the right one: shape and grey-level produce pop-out, but their conjunction does not.

Experiments in psychology have used these features to perform the following pre-attentive visual tasks:

1. Target detection: users attempt to detect rapidly and accurately the presence or absence of a "target" element with a unique visual feature within a field of distractor elements.

2. Boundary detection: users attempt to detect rapidly and accurately a texture boundary between two groups of elements, where all the elements in each group have a common visual property.

3. Counting: users attempt to count or estimate the number of elements in a display that share a unique visual feature.

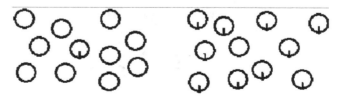

Figure 3. Example of pre-attentive task (left) and attentive task (right), serial detection is required to look for the plain circle.

Figure 4. Regions composed by two different textures. In the first two examples, the texture partition is quite evident.

Another set of problems arises when introducing time. A practical application is in the visualization of data as soon as they are generated from real-time applications. The goal is to perform data analysis tasks (such as detection of data groups and boundaries, target detection, and estimation) rapidly and accurately on a dynamic sequence of data frames. Healey [12] provides some behavioral experiment on temporal boundary detection and temporal target detection, using as practical applications a visualization system designed to help analyze results from salmon tracking simulations and the visualization of slice data from medical imaging systems.

3. A Counterexample

We consider now a counterexample (Figure 5) to understand how data visualizations can be made more effective considering the visual preattentive features of the human perceptual system.

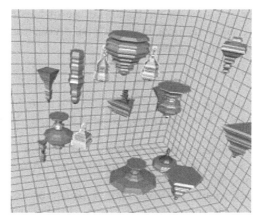

Figure 5. An example of multidimensional financial visualization that does not take into account the eye preattentive capabilities (image courtesy Mark Mason - AVS UK).

Each glyph represents a different mutual fund spatially organized by Fund Company, fund sector type, etc. Each floating 3D glyph shows a green/red color-coded and shape coded price history silhouette. The number of sides of the glyph maps another discrete parameter, and the white net another binary value. In total the visualization try to display three continuous, one discrete, one binary variable plus a continuous and one discrete timeseries for each data point.

It is immediately evident that it is difficult to extract patterns and base decisions on this visualization especially if imagining this tool used in a highly stressful situation like a trading room.

Besides the problems related to feature interference, there are the problems related to space perception on a two-dimensional screen: occlusion, relative size perception due to perspective projection.

It is much better to display the various data dimensions using 2D scatter plot that encodes two parameters as spatial axis and one or two as glyph features. This setup enables the visualization of correlations between two to four variables for each plot. Obviously more plots should be used to display all the possible correlations between the various parameters.

Another problem with this visualization is that probably has been developed considering the technical capabilities of the tool only. Instead, a good strategy to develop visualizations is to analyze what is the goal the user is pursuing and defining which cognitive task this visualization is supposed to help. With high probability, this analysis phase would cut down considerably on the number of 2D scatter plots needed.

4. Future Works

We are currently investigating the combined use of important and commonly used pre-attentive visual features, in order to build visualization tools that allow more effective visual analysis tasks.

References

1. B. Bauer, P. Jolicoeur, W. B. Cowan, *Visual search for colour targets that are or are not linearly-separable from distractors,* Vision Research, **36,** 1439–1446 (1996).
2. B. Bauer, P. Jolicoeur, W. B. Cowan, *The linearly separability effect in color visual search: Ruling out the additive color hypothesis,* Perception & Psychophysics, **60,** 1083–1093 (1998).
3. J. Beck, K. Prazdny, A. Rosenfeld, *A theory of textural segmentation,* Human and Machine Vision, J. Beck, K. Prazdny, Rosenfeld, Eds. Academic Press, New York, New York, 1983, pp. 1-39.

4. V. Cantoni, M. Marinaro, A. Petrosino, editors, *Visual attention mechanisms*, Kluwer (2002).
5. W. Colin, *Information visualization: perception for design*, Morgan Kaufmann (2004).
6. J. Driver, P. McLeod, Z. Dienes, *Motion coherence and conjunction search: Implications for guided search theory*, Perception & Psychophysics, **51**, 1 79–85 (1992).
7. M. D'Zmura, *Color in visual search*, Vision Research, **31**, 6, 951–966 (1991).
8. J. T. Enns, *Seeing textons in context*. Perception & Psychophysics, **39**, 143–147 (1986).
9. J. T. Enns, *The promise of finding effective geometric codes,* Proceedings Visualization 1990, San Francisco, California, 389–390.
10. J. T. Enns, *Three-dimensional features that pop out in visual search*. Visual Search, Taylor & Francis, New York, 37–45 (1990).
11. C. G.Healey, K. S. Booth, J. T. Enns, *Harnessing preattentive processes for multivariate data visualization*. Proceedings Graphics Interface 1993, Toronto, Canada, 107–117.
12. C. G. Healey, K. S. Booth, J. T. Enns, *Visualizing real-time multivariate data using preattentive processing*, ACM Transactions on Modeling and Computer Simulation, **5**, 3 190–221 (1995).
13. C. G. Healey, *Choosing effective colours for data visualization,* Proceedings Visualization 1996, San Francisco, California, 263–270.
14. C. G. Healey, J. T. Enns, *Building perceptual textures to visualize multidimensional datasets*, Proceedings Visualization 1998, Research Triangle Park, North Carolina, 111–118.
15. C. G. Healey, J. T. Enns, *Large datasets at a glance: Combining textures and colors in scientific visualization,* IEEE Transactions on Visualization and Computer Graphics, **5**, 2, 145–167 (1999).
16. C. G. Healey, *Formalizing artistic techniques and scientific visualization for painted renditions of complex information spaces,* Proceedings International Joint Conference on Artificial Intelligence IJCAI 2001, Seattle, Washington, 371–376.
17. C. G. Healey, J. T. Enns, *Perception and painting: A search for effective, engaging visualizations,* IEEE Computer Graphics & Applications, **22**, 2, 10–15 (2002).
18. C. G. Healey, J. T. Enns, L. G. Tateosian, M. Remple, *Perceptually-based brush strokes for nonphotorealistic visualization*. ACM Transactions on Graphics, **23**, 1, 64–96 (2004).
19. B. Julész, *Foundations of Cyclopean Perception*. University of Chicago Press, Chicago, Illinois, 1971.
20. B. Julész, J. R. Bergen, *Textons, the fundamental elements in preattentive vision and the perception of textures*. Bell System Technical Journal, **62**, 6, 1619–1645 (1983).

21. M. Kawai, K. Uchikawa, H. Ujike, *Influence of color category on visual search.* Annual Meeting of the Association for Research in Vision and Ophthalmology, Fort Lauderdale, Florida, 1995, 2991.
22. G. Liu, C. G. Healey, J. T. Enns, *Target detection and localization in visual search: A dual systems perspective,* Perception & Psychophysics, **65**, 5, 678–694 (2003).
23. A. L. Nagy, R. R. Sanchez, *Critical color differences determined with a visual search task,* Journal of the Optical Society of America A, **7**, 7, 1209–1217 (1990).
24. A. L. Nagy, R. R. Sanchez, T. C. Hughes, *Visual search for color differences with foveal and peripheral vision,* Journal of the Optical Society of America A, **7**, 10, 1995–2001 (1990).
25. K. Nakayama, G. H. Silverman, *Serial and parallel processing of visual feature conjunctions,* Nature, **320**, 264–265 (1986).
26. D. Sagi, B. Julész, *Detection versus discrimination of visual orientation,* Perception, **14**, 619–628 (1985).
27. D. Sagi, B. Julész, *The "Where" and "What" of vision.* Science, *228*, 1217–1219 (1985).
28. L. Trick, Z. Pylyshyn, *Why are small and large numbers enumerated differently? A limited capacity preattentive stage in vision,* Psychology Review, **101**, 80–102 (1994).
29. A. Triesman, G. Gelade, *A feature-integration theory of attention,* Cognitive Psychology, **12**, 97–136 (1980).
30. A. Triesman, J. Souther, *Illusory words: The roles of attention and top-down constraints in conjoining letters to form words,* Journal of Experimental Psychology: Human Perception & Performance, **12**, 107–141 (1986).
31. A. Triesman, S. Gormican, *Feature analysis in early vision: Evidence from search asymmetries,* Psychological Review, **95**, 1, 15–48, (1988).
32. E. R. Tufte, *The Visual Display of Quantitative Information,* Graphics (1983)
33. C. Weigle, W. G. Emigh, G. Liu, R. M. Taylor, J. T. Enns, C. G. Healey, *Oriented texture slivers: A technique for local value estimation of multiple scalar fields,* Proceedings Graphics Interface 2000, Montréal, Canada, 2000, 163–170.
34. J. M. Wolfe, S. L. Franzel, *Binocularity and visual search,* Perception & Psychophysics, **44**, 81–93 (1988).
35. J. M. Wolfe, S. R. Friedman-Hill, M. I. Stewart, K. M. O'Connell, *The role of categorization in visual search for orientation,* Journal of Experimental Psychology: Human Perception & Performance, **18**, 1, 34–49 (1992).

INTEGRATING HUMAN AND MACHINE PERCEPTION TO REVERSE-ENGINEER THE HUMAN VISION SYSTEM

ROBERTA PIRODDI, MARIA PETROU

Centre for Vision, Speech and Signal Processing,
University of Surrey, Guildford GU2 7XH, United Kingdom

In this paper, we provide some examples of integration of human and machine perception, derived from a specific research project that aims at emulating the human vision system.

1. Introduction

Reverse Engineering is the activity of disassembling a complex system, whether it is hardware or software, in order to analyse its parts, understand their relationship and workings and finally replicate its functions into a new system or product. In the case of reverse engineering the human vision system [15], the method is that of subdividing the human vision system into functional areas for the purpose of analysing and simulating the different parts separately. Then, a process of synthesis is needed to understand the mutual relationship between the parts and identify the system as a whole. The final aim is that of obtaining a global blueprint of the human visual system that may be used to help medical practitioners to devise ways to cure patients suffering from visual impairment, and computer scientists to develop better artificial vision systems.

Why reverse engineering the human visual system is needed to support the medical community? Let us take as an example the history of the development of an artificial retina. An artificial retina is a prosthetic aid designed to integrate (not substitute) the human visual perception, in case of failure of a component of it.

The first examples of retinal implants do not try to simulate the retina, but only to stimulate it. Such stimulation consists of electrical impulses similar to those produced by the photoreceptors. The signal is directly transmitted to the ganglion cells and from there to the optical nerve [7]. This solution bypasses all the preprocessing power exerted by the five cellular layers of the retina.

A first approximation, in which this biological interface is taken into consideration, is given by sub-retinal implants [18,4]. Sub-retinal implants stimulate the bipolar cells, allowing the lens to focus directly onto the chip. Because the sub-retinal implants are located between the first layer of the retina, the photoreceptors, and the last layer of the retina, the ganglion cells, such devices can simulate part of the preprocessing functions of the retina. Going even further on the visual pathway, the electrical stimulation of the visual cortex had been pioneered already by the late 1970s, but only recently such a device has been tested on patients [5]. However, it has been pointed out recently that the way to produce meaningful stimulation is to understand the processes of healthy retinas and then simulate them [2]. This is the novel idea that supports the concept of retinotopic devices [2].

Understanding how the human visual system works as a global system may also benefit the design of new artificial vision systems. Biological systems have many desirable characteristics, like robustness to noise and adaptivity to changes in the environment. All these features may be learnt and incorporated in artificial designs.

In this paper, we wish to give concrete examples of integration of human and artificial perception, in the quest to reverse engineer the human vision system. We shall show examples of overlapping of problems and needs between biological and artificial disciplines. We shall show how the understanding of biological systems can support novel solutions in computer vision, and we shall show how we may use mathematical paradigms to provide tentative explanations and/or simulations of biological problems.

2. Examples of Integration

Before going into details of particular functional areas of the human vision system, let us have a brief, global view of the pathway followed by the visual signal. In this way it will be easier to locate the examples provided below. The light signal from the external world is first perceived by the retina, which constitutes the pavement of the eye. The retina is formed by five cellular layers: the photoreceptors, the horizontal cells, the bipolar cells, the amacrine cells and the ganglion cells. The ganglion cells transmit the signal to the optical nerve. The signal travels first to the Lateral Geniculate Nucleus to finally hit the Visual Cortex, located in the occipital region of the brain. The Visual Cortex is divided into a number of functional areas. Each area analyses a particular aspect of the signal, for example colour, motion and shape. Each areas is also widely connected to many others through both feed-forward and feed-back connections. We are interested in this work in the first and biggest area of the visual cortex, which is called V1. This part of the cortex is sensitive to bars and edges at different orientations. Higher functional areas perform the integration of simple characteristics of the signal, for example for the purpose of object recognition. These processes are strongly influenced by the mechanisms of attention. More details about the structure of the Human Visual System may be found, among others, in [3].

2.1. *The spatial structure of the retina and the problem of irregular sampling*

The cells composing the retina do not have a regular distribution on a rectangular grid, like the digital images, that are made out of pixels. Their concentration diminishes with the distance from the fovea, the part of the retina which follows the focus of attention. The radial dependence is not a regular one either, and every individual possesses a special spatial pattern, personalised like a finger-print. Moreover, the number of the cells present in the first cellular layer, the photoreceptors, is much bigger than the number of cells in the last layer, the ganglion cells. Therefore, there is compression of the information that takes part between the first and the last cellular layer. The maximum rate of information is preserved only on the very focus of the attention and on an irregular substrate. And still a human viewer perceives the world as a continuum.

The problem of irregular distribution of signal samples does not occur only with biological vision. In fields like telecommunications, geoscience, remote sensing, astrophysics, medical imaging, oceanography, irregular and corrupted signals occur and have to be meaningfully analysed. Nevertheless, image processing continues to treat only regular images on a grid and, if irregularity appears, the solution is to interpolate the missing samples and continue as if the signal had always been a regularly sampled one.

In order to be able to interface with retinotopic devices, which present the same irregular structure as the retina, and perform image processing on their output, it is necessary to find ways to perform the usual tasks (like image reconstruction or edge detection) directly onto irregular samples. We need to develop a new irregular image processing.

We may learn to perform irregular image processing by looking at what other disciplines have produced and adapt these techniques to the two dimensional realm. Following this idea, we performed a comparative study of techniques deducted from varying disciplines, which we adapted for the purpose of application to digital images [13]. We found that two techniques, namely Iterative Interpolation [1,16] and Normalized Convolution [9] provide the best reconstruction results. Normalized Convolution provides better results for sampling ratios lower than fifteen percent (that is cases when less than fifteen percent of the information is used to reconstruct the original signal); while Iterative Interpolation provides sharper results for sampling ratios higher than fifteen percent. Examples of reconstructions obtained with the two method are shown in Figure 1. More detailed information may be found in [14].

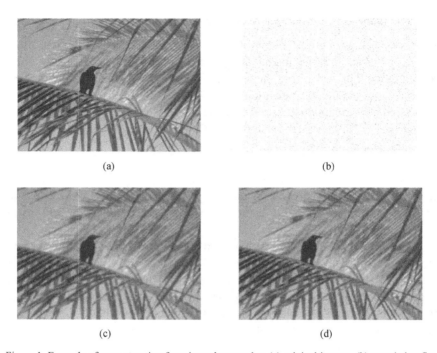

(a)   (b)

(c)   (d)

Figure 1. Example of reconstruction from irregular samples: (a) original images, (b) sampled at five percent, (c) reconstructed from (b) using Normalized Convolution and (d) reconstructed from (b) using Iterative Interpolation.

Normalized Convolution in particular is a very interesting technique, since it is direct, fast and takes into consideration not just the value and location of the sample, but also its certainty. We found that an extension of Normalized Convolution, the Normalized Differential Convolution [17], provides extremely good edge detection on irregular samples. In Figure 2c and 2d, we show the gradient estimation obtained on the sampled image in Figure 2b, obtained sampling Figure 2a at a sampling ratio of ten percent. In Figure 2e and 2f respectively, we show the edges extracted with the Normalized Differential Convolution, with the use of the original filter presented in [17] and with the Canny filter, in the optimal formulation given in [12]. With this example, we show that the Normalized Differential Convolution may be applied flexibly to a number of filters, with excellent results. Details of this technique are provided in [14]. Given the performance obtained in such fundamental tasks with so little information, the idea of irregular sampling, taken from biological structures, might provide an alternative solution to the problem of image compression.

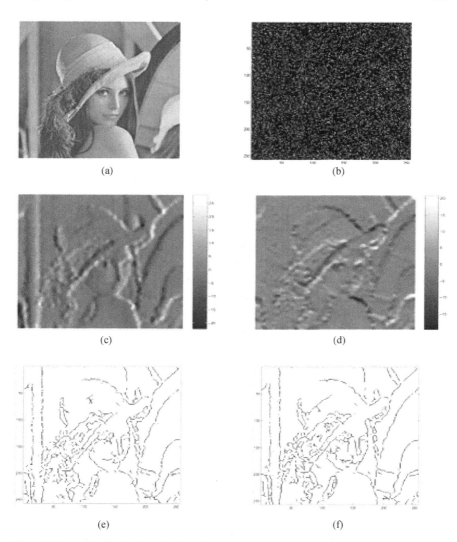

Figure 2. Example of edge detection from irregular samples: (a) original image, (b) sub-sampling mask containing the position of ten percent of the samples (pixels), (c) gradient estimated along the horizontal direction using Normalized Differential Convolution, (d) gradient estimated along the vertical direction using the Normalized Differential Convolution, (e) edges produced by the application of filter in [17] and (f) edges produced by the application of the Canny filter [12].

2.2. *A unique saliency map from pre-attentive neuronal interactions*

The common approach to building saliency maps in image processing is that of computing a number of feature maps, each according to a specific feature and/or orientation, and then combining them into a single, master saliency map. This approach, however, does not take into consideration the psychological and neurological evidence.

From the psychological point of view, there are patterns that pop-out effortlessly, pre-attentively to the human perception, regardless of the particular feature considered. In [11], the neurological connections in layers 2 and 3 of V1 have been studied to formulate a model according to which, regardless of the single cell tuning to a particular feature, the firing rate of the cells reports only the saliency of the feature.

This study concentrates on the presence of two opposed behaviours, as shown in Figure 3. The pyramidal cells produce an excitatory signal depending on the extension of their receptive field. However, the horizontal connections established by the interneurons, exert an inhibitory signal, which collects information from the surrounding cells. This causes the signal to be related to a wider area than that of the receptive field only.

Studying the particular neural connections, some rules can be produced [10]. The response of the cell is weak if the surrounding cells respond to the same orientation. The same response is at its strongest in case neighbouring cells respond to perpendicular stimuli to that of the cell considered. However, if a smooth boundary is present, then the firing rate increases again.

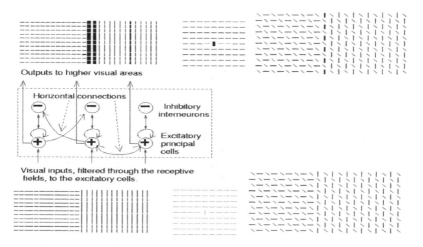

Figure 3. V1 produces a saliency map by highlighting perceptually important regions. Taken from [11] .

We wanted to see whether this theory can help in the task of edge detection. We performed a comparison between the Canny edge detector and the saliency map obtained with the model in [10]. Here we present an application to medical image analysis, shown in Figure 4.

It is possible to see that meaningful boundaries present themselves with higher impact in the case of the saliency map. This model is therefore advantageous in the case of typical image processing applications, because it is very economical in terms of number of features to be computed and unambiguous in terms of criteria for feature combination.

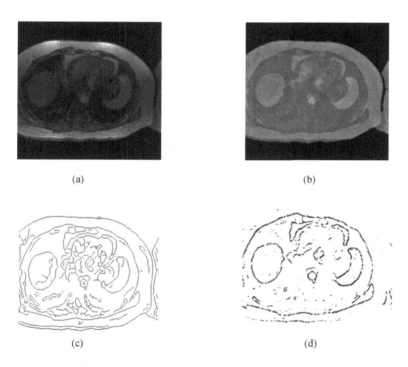

Figure 4. Application to the saliency map to medical imaging: (a) an original medical image, (b) pre-processed image produced from (a), (c) edges detected with the use of Canny edge detector, (d) saliency map produced with the use of the biologically motivated model in [11]. Pictures courtesy of H. Ibrahim and M. Petrou, University of Surrey.

2.3. The trace transform and its application to pre-attentive irregular texture ranking

We have seen in Section 2.1 that image processing is usually performed on regular grids, but this is not the case in the human visual system. Another task we are interested to investigate is texture ranking on irregular grids. Texture ranking indicates the function of classification of different textural patterns in terms of their similarity. In [16], the model chosen to try to explain this phenomenon is the trace transform. The trace transform [8] operates along lines that criss-cross the image. Along these lines it computes a number of functionals of choice, which can be sensitive or insensitive to linear transformations.

Each line is fully defined by two parameters. The trace transform plots the value computed along each tracing line as a function of the parameters of the line. This way it creates 2D image representations alternative to the classical one consisting of values at sampling points (the pixels). Each such representation may be reduced to 1D by computing a functional along batches of parallel lines. This allows the representation of the image by a string of numbers, one for each direction chosen. Finally, computing a third functional from this string of numbers allows one to produce a single number, a feature, that characterises the image. Such features may be used to characterise a given texture. An example of a texture image and its trace transform is shown in Figure 5.

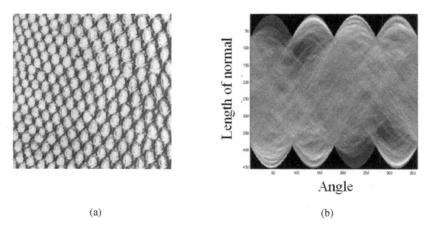

(a)   (b)

Figure 5. (a) A texture sample and (b) its trace transform.

Why might this model be relevant to human vision? The *tremor* of the eye is a movement that criss-crosses the field of view of the eye in a similar way to that of the trace transform. This movement is performed with 40-120 cycles per second and amplitude of about 1 degree [16]. We may formulate the hypothesis that during the straight line scanning of the image in the fovea area, the information is transformed according to specific functionals and integrated along those lines.

The trace transform allows one to perform image recognition from values of the scene along lines. This bypasses the problem of irregular sampling, as lines may be formed from sampling points either they are on a regular or an irregular grid. From the algorithmic point of view, such lines may be identified with the help of the Hough transform.

The trace transform was applied to extract features in order to classify a set of 112 natural textures from the Brodatz database, irregularly sampled with a sampling ratio of forty-five percent, using a retinotopic sampling pattern. The classification accuracy obtained, over all the parameter settings used to tune the similarity function, is shown in Figure 6. With less than thirty percent of the available samples, the classification accuracy is between seventy and sixty percent, independently of parameter setting.

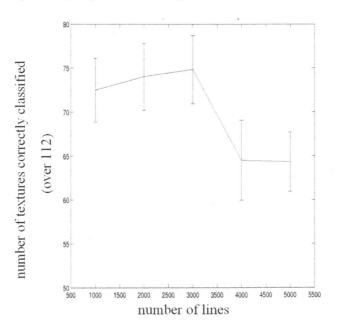

Figure 6. Classification accuracy in case of retinotopically sampled textures. The results are averages over all parameter settings.

3. Conclusions

In this paper we have seen how the needs of human and artificial vision may overlap and how both human and artificial vision can provide useful paradigms to better understand their tasks or address specific problems.

In the case of irregular sampling, this phenomenon occurs in both the biological and artificial domain. Solutions found in the artificial domain can be exploited to simulate biological behaviour. In the same way, irregularity is used in the biological organisms for compression purposes. This is a fertile idea to be incorporated in the case of image compression problems.

The study of specific neuronal connections in V1 offers an economic and meaningful alternative to feature selection, reduction and integration for preattentive mechanisms. This might be incorporated in image processing solutions as well. So this is a field where artificial perception can learn from the biological one.

Finally, in the case of the trace transform, we have seen how mathematical tools may be used to advance a verification hypothesis of biological phenomena and simulate them.

Acknowledgements

This work was funded by the Research Councils of the United Kingdom of Great Britain and Northern Ireland, under the research grant number GR/R87642.

The authors wish to thank: J. Ng and A. Bharath, at Imperial College London, for providing the implementation of the Normalized Convolution, Z. Li, at University College London, for providing the illustration of the saliency maps in Figure 3 and H. Ibrahim, at the University of Surrey, for the implementation of the saliency theory of Z. Li.

References

1. J.J Benedetto and M.J. Frazier, editors. *Wavelets: Mathematics and Applications*, CRC Press (1994).
2. K. Boahen. The retinotopic approach: pixel parallel adaptive amplification, filtering and quantisation. *Analog Integrated Circuits and Signal Processing*, 13:53-68 (1997).
3. V. Bruce and P. Green. *Visual Perception*. Lawrence Erlbaum Associates (1990).
4. A. Chow, V. Chow, K. Packo, J. Pollack, G. Peyman, and R. Schuchard. The artificial silicon retina microchip for the treatment of vision loss from retinitis pigmentosa. *Archives of Ophthalmology*, 122(4):460-469 (2004).

5. W. Dobelle. Artificial vision for the blind by electrical stimulation of the visual cortex. *Neurosurgery*, 5(4):521-527 (1979).
6. K. Groechenig. A discrete theory of irregular sampling. *Linear Algebra and its Applications*, 193:129-150 (1993).
7. M. Humayun, E. de Juan, and G. Dagnelie. Visual perception elicited by electrical stimulation of retina in blind humans. *Archives of Ophthalmology*, 114:40-46 (1996).
8. A. Kadyrov and M. Petrou, The trace transform and its applications. *IEEE Transactions on Pattern Analysis and Machine Intelligence*, 23(8):811-828 (2001).
9. H. Knutsson and C.-F. Westin. Normalized and differential convolution: Methods for interpolation and filtering of incomplete and uncertain data. In *IEEE Conference on Computer Vision and Pattern Recognition*, 515-523 (1993).
10. Z. Li. Visual segmentation by contextual influences via intracortical interactions in primary visual cortex. *Network: Computation in Neural Systems*, 10(2): 187-212 (1999).
11. Z. Li. A saliency map in primary visual cortex. *Trends in Cognitive Sciences*, 6(1): 9-16, 2002.
12. M. Petrou. The differentiating filter approach to edge detection. In *Advances in Electronics and Electron Physics*, 88: 297-345. Academic Press (1994).
13. M. Petrou, R. Piroddi, and S. Chandra. Irregularly sampled scenes. In L. Bruzzone (editor), *SPIE Image and Signal Processing for Remote Sensing X*, SPIE-CD 5573 (2004).
14. R. Piroddi and M. Petrou, Dealing with irregular samples, In P.W. Hawkes (editor), advances in *Imaging and Electron Physics*, 132: 109-165, Elsevier (2004).
15. Reverse Engineering the Human Vision System: A Basic Technology Project. Web-Page URL: www.ee.surrey.ac.uk/Basic/.
16. A. Talebpour, M. Petrou, and A. Kadyrov, Texture Analysis using the trace transform, submitted to *Pattern Analysis and Applications*, Springer.
17. C.-F. Westin and H. Knutsson. Processing incomplete and uncertain data using subspace methods. In *IAPR International Conference on Pattern Recognition*, 171-173 (1994).
18. E. Zenner, S. Weiss, A. Stett, B. Bruner, V.-P. Gabel, M. Graf, H. Graf, H. Haemmerle, B. Hoeffinger, K. Kobuch, K.-D. Miliczek, W. Nisch, H. Sachs, and M. Stelze. Are subretinal microphotodiodes suitable as a replacement for degenerated photoreceptors? In *Retinal Degenerative Diseases and Experimental Therapy*, 497-505. Kluwer Academic/Plenum Press (1999).

SITUATED VISION: A STEP FURTHER TOWARDS AUTONOMOUS SYSTEMS

BERTRAND ZAVIDOVIQUE, ROGER REYNAUD

Université PARIS SUD, Institut d'Electronique Fondamentale, Département AXIS
F91405 – Orsay, Cedex, France
{bertrand.zavidovique,roger.reynaud}@ief.u-psud.fr

This chapter is about vision to make systems more autonomous. We parallel two aspects of the current evolution of System-Perception: more ambitious yet coherent tasks tightly rely on more abstract description and control. As vision is likely to be a major and complex sensory modality for machines as it is for most animals, we concentrate our development on it. In the first part we show how thinking to systems helped to better pose vision problems and solve them in a useful manner. That is the "active vision" trend that we explain and illustrate. Along the same line, the necessity for anticipation further shows, leading to a first definition of "situated vision". The second part deals with how to design systems able to achieve such vision. We show from a few examples how architectural descriptions evolve and better fit important features to grasp –a model– in view of more efficient control towards intelligence. Inner communication flows are better be controlled than local tasks that should be assumed completed efficiently enough in all cases. We conclude with a plausible sketch of a system to be experimented on in situations that require some autonomy.

There are several facets to system intelligence. Most popular ones relate to the tasks that systems can complete, to the evolving situations they can cope with or their ability to versatile self-configuration from adaptability to learning. All deal with the goals of the system, meaning its properties when being observed at work. A less obvious feature for a system to be intelligent refers more to technological yet fundamental aspects: it concerns all ways data and then information can flow across and between parts of it, being stored and transformed along the process. It deals with the internal ability of the system to be described, thus built.

It is well known that prehistoric monsters such as brontosaurus still had a brain as big as an orange for the global size of half a dozen buses and were likely very slow and ill-coordinated due to the difficulty for messages to go from head to toes. On the other hand, considering a philharmonic orchestra of comparative size, it is not enough that members play right respecting the tempo and not producing wrong notes. At some point for the audience to start being thrilled, performers need to really play together and make music: that refers to some chemistry extremely hard to explain except for the key role that communication plays into it up to real communion. At that stage even dissonance are not a problem and may accrue the pleasure (see Figure 1).

Figure 1. Two intelligent systems to different degrees.

From a system point of view an orchestra is a parallel machine that transforms a given set of human energies into one melodious – to say the least – sound, under control of a distributed full score and a conductor's will. The eye should obviously play a major part beside the main sensor for the task that is the ear. Some members, the operators inside this parallel machine, may have more ancient instruments than others' with different timbre then, some may be slightly slower or faster to react; they likely have different feelings about the piece of music to play and its rendering, one could have a tooth-ache that day, etc. But in the end they will sound like one instrument extremely advanced and complex compared to any component (see Figure 2).

How do they do that? They use any suitable sensor at their disposal not only to listen to the output air or read music lines, but also to understand and locally compensate for any variation that would not contribute to the goal: ears to track each slight variation in the local output by themselves and their group while getting a more global impression, eyes to check on the neighbors' attitude indicative of the rhythm or on the conductor's pose and gesture. Even more than that, they keep communicating through their own body expression, eye contact or sound modulations e.g. in burst or intensity: not only do they perform an active perception on the sense they search for every pertinent piece of information to use, but they help others do that. Not to forget that rehearsal got every member used to the other and to the conductor's message that codes the ultimate goal of the system: the training made easier interpretation of all internal signals in building a common more abstract language (see Figure 3).

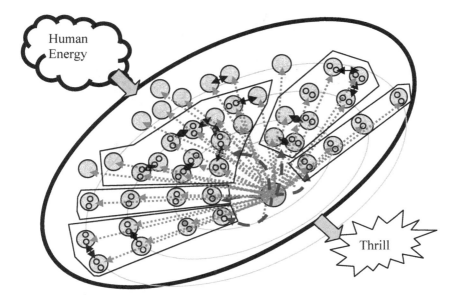

Figure 2. An architecture view to the orchestra.

Now, the question in this chapter is also how we can describe such a system. With a bit of "reverse engineering": firstly, how does the conductor manage to control it, and based on which representation? Secondly how do we relate the output – a pleasure to stem from the harmony – to the system description including its controller? It becomes understandable that a learning method for any given instrument in the orchestra will not help that much, neither would the understanding of the physics of sound-making that varies a lot from brass to percussions or strings, nor would the knowledge of the precise physiological health state of the second violin etc. At that stage there is no other way for description – that is modeling and the first step towards efficient control – than to assume that any local part of the system will complete its own task at best and that this best is enough. Would it be only because if it is not the case, the goal is likely never to be achieved and then any optimization or control becomes useless! Conversely, a description focusing on information flows and retaining local efficiency gauges only should be more suitable for behavior control. The denser and more abstract the description, the higher level the control (see Figure 4).

Figure 3. On the interest of off-line training.

Eventually, describing a system that reaches comparative a level of coordination to the service of a given performance cannot be in terms of what each component does right or wrong. Again, at this level of complexity, one needs to assume every part fulfils its task satisfactorily as a necessary prerequisite. The supplement of activity allowing the behavior to be perceived as intelligent is all a matter of inner communication and control. The more abstract system description then fits the more abstract and general system activity: indeed explaining how a body would endeavor to survive in all circumstances is better done in terms of running (fast motion), hiding (environmental fusion) or fighting (strong reaction) subject to perception, rather than in terms of the precise moves of each joint of each member in the 3-D geometric task-related space transformed from the 4-D virtual sensory space.

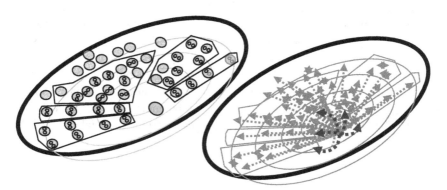

Figure 4. Dual views to the orchestra's architecture.

Building on such considerations, the present chapter parallels both aspects of the current evolution of System-Perception: more ambitious yet coherent tasks tightly bound to more abstract description and control. As vision is likely to be a major and complex sensory modality for machines as it is for most animals, we first concentrate our development on it. In the first part we show how thinking to systems helped to better pose vision problems and solve them in a useful manner. Following that line, the necessity for anticipation is put forward, leading to a first definition of situated vision. The second part deals with how to design systems able to achieve such vision, more generally embedded into Perception. We show from a few examples how sensor fusion architecture descriptions evolve and fit better important features to grasp –a model–in view of more efficient control towards intelligence. The chapter concludes with a sketch of a system to be experimented on in situations that require some autonomy.

1. The Evolution of Machine Vision

1.1. *The Historical Perspective*

In the 80's, vision systems are mostly oriented towards the environment reconstruction, mainly geometric. 3-D modeling is then central in all these systems before any decision is to be taken (moving cameras, changing parameters...): this is the MIT's fashion, after Marr's theory of early vision and primal sketch, to ground the reconstruction on shape from-X (contour, shading, texture) and on optical flow for motion. Note that no actually running system ever came out of this, and that all known real systems (see for instance [1] to [23]) did proceed in a quasi opposite way: the 3-D configuration was somewhat of a perception/action loop by-product to be used if necessary. Such an apparent miracle stems from the active way vision gets involved in these latter systems' overall behavior.

Indeed, most vision and hence perception problems are ill posed in the Hadamard's sense because they aim at inverting multiple projections: on a focal plane by sensing, on integers by sampling, on features by segmenting, etc. Some others as navigation in a rigid world are well posed but highly unstable. Rather than regularizing with constraints like smoothness, somewhat questionable on variables measured from the scene, engineers would constrain the sensors that have to be mastered anyway. Then Aloimonos [24] in 1988 started to formalize the idea and successfully checked its validity on four fashionable questions at that time: shape from shading, from contours, from texture (ill-posed in their passive setting), and structure from motion (unstable in its passive setting). A similar effort is later due to Clark who computes a depth map in 1992, by stereo photometry where the light source moves in a controlled way. The concept of active perception considered in the chapter is closer to Bajcsy's in 1985 [25] and to our own ideas [26],[27],[28] of solving problems by a strategy of sensor control: that implies explicit perceptive goals and selection criteria. Nowadays several trends have been classified in this approach:

Active vision: a rather theoretical analysis of the vision process originated by Aloimonos to optimize visual or visually guided tasks [24],[29],[30]. Structure from controlled motion [31],[32] belongs to this category in so far as cameras' moves help to optimize the 3-D reconstruction.

Active perception: a study of perception strategies, including sensor and signal processing cooperation, to achieve knowledge about the environment better [33],[34],[35]. The concept extends up to all sensor fusion where information gathers from several points of view, several physical principles of sensors, and several time steps. Other examples are trying to define strategies [36],[37], designing supervisors [38], or studying the impact of acquisition uncertainty on feedback [39].

Animate vision [40]: based on human perception analysis [41],[42], it aims at mimicking fixation and gaze control. Ballard's objective is to optimize the algorithm complexity, and to that effect, one major idea is to consider exocentric rather than egocentric coordinates that are invariant with the observer's movements. In [43], [44], [45], [46] one can find additional results of the category.

Purposive vision: In [47], another point of departure is the evidence that most vision systems have to answer precise questions and about a limited number of known tasks. In such a context, only pertaining information relative to the running task needs to be extracted. A designer has to ask the following questions in order: to what aim is the system built? Which knowledge is needed to reach the goal? How does one get this knowledge? An extended analysis and discussion of what seems a re-constructionist approach again lays in [48],[49],[50].

1.2. *First Applications*

There is no doubt that technology helps in this evolution by miniaturizing, then accelerating, sensors and processors, and by varying the underlying physical phenomena to provide additional degrees of freedom (e.g. adjusting geometry and optics concurrently). At that stage, precise and complete modeling of all components in a perception system is seldom feasible. Thus, for system identification at least, experimenting cannot be avoided. The key role of technology in the success of the active perception approach over the last decade is evidenced by an explosive growth of binocular or trinocular heads to experiment in the sole domain of localization and tracking by triangulation or disparity based or other techniques. [51] up to [67]!

To further understand the exact level of realism enabled by these techniques, we list a few representative examples in different applications ranked by increasing complexity.

Quantitative surface description: position-control of the optical axis gives access to geometric surface features (e.g. local curvature and principal axes) from multiple views, thanks to the Blaschke's theorem [68] [69].

3-D reconstruction with occlusions: a hybrid sensor made of a laser rigidly coupled with a camera swipes a plane. Its known geometry gives access to the depth of all object points in the scene. Occlusions generate blind zones in two ways: the *laser* beam does not reach any surface, or its reflection does not reach the *camera*. A plane rotation solves the first type while a rotation of the support inside the plane solves the second type. In that case, the movement's optimization is purely spatial (no idea of saccade or any other time minimization).

Visual system control: vision may serve a classical feedback in two ways [70]:

- Look and move: the relative position of the camera respective to an object (opportune landmark) is measured out of the processed image and taken for the input. Then, the difference "estimation/objective" is minimized in moving the camera.

- Visual servoing: the objective deals directly with extracted image features (for instance the camera is moved to align specific points of interest). This technique is faster, but it requires the interaction-matrix mapping image features on to camera moves, which may not be fully computable.

The research in that domain is still ongoing about feature efficiency, control laws, and robustness.

Indirect search: autonomy implies for robots to localize objects of intermediate or temporary interest considering the current phase of a mission. Wide-angle cameras either do not help for small objects or distort, and narrow angle cameras may take long to scan the whole field of view. Wixson [71],[72] proposed a general search scheme based on spatial relations between intermediate significant objects, easy to spot in low resolution, and small or less obvious objects to be found only in high resolution. Finding the first one thanks to its size or color will restrict the translation/rotation of the narrow angle device. Efficiencies have been compared, and gains in time to find the target can be as large as eight. More structural relations, based on physics for instance, were considered as well [73].

Tracking information from interpretation: TEA1 [74], [75], and then d (for dynamic)-TEA1, answer questions of the kind "Who is coming for dinner?" on planar static scenes. If a distinguished guest is expected, several glasses are set for each person. To confirm a given conjecture, the system selectively gathers image data in variable resolution and processes them accordingly. A priori knowledge is coded as {P(object$_1$ in x,y / object$_2$ in u,v), object hierarchies, dependence inter elementary actions} into Bayes nets. Full interpretation is completed in 5 steps:

- Checking the list of actions
- Exhibiting the most suitable one (informative gain/cost)
- Firing the action
- Updating nodes in the causal nets
- Iterating up to reach a predefined confidence in the answer

These latter examples were among the most sophisticated. It confirms that the better balance between processing and control actually enables systems to escape the curse of prior environment reconstruction. This is replaced by perception-action loops as in visual feedback or indirect search. Then resource allocation together with technology (e.g. supply independence, miniaturization, or networking) makes them more versatile. Obviously, though intuitively, they can answer much higher-level perception requests (finding glasses on a table takes more than mere segmentation) and they already secure a large variety of local but more general decisions (assessing slopes, finding sub-paths, etc.).

1.3. *Towards more Advanced Applications*

Yet, no such system suggests real autonomy: the robot skills provided so far seem again too sparse and likely to be operating in isolation. Whether it is purposive or animate vision, the goal seems to lower algorithm – or system – complexity more than to augment the system ability considering a given set of modules. The situated vision aims at such control to making resources communicate better. Likely a direct consequence of the lack of global optimization, most operations completed at this level remain robot centered: the machine profits by its own moves to know better a static environment.

To give a temporal example, finding by itself intermediate landmarks is a significant improvement but what happens if there is no other interesting object than a mobile one, or if the interest bound to the scene or to the very perceptive task stems from the movement? Objects' motions are then part of the on-set, and assuming the robot tracks a moving object, it could never catch it. The difference between active and situated vision in this case is looking where the target *is*, versus looking at the location, and more generally situation, the target *will be* in.

These ten last years, functional modules exhibit increased adaptability, generality, and semantic level. Two examples among many illustrate the progress: in Munich, where the very first autonomous car was built [1 to 6], the current generation tackles Expectations, Multi focal and Saccadic gaze control; in Oxford the ConDensAtion algorithm supports improved tracking through a more general representation of probability, akin to Kalman with multi-modal conditional densities [76],[77], (see also [33],[70],[78],[79], and further results on probability extent attempts including fuzziness, evidence, etc.). Components get more adaptive along with technology, systems do not.

Then both at the same time, modules are fulfilling there tasks in a satisfactory manner and a more global optimization is required to go beyond the present level of intelligence. The stress being put on communication, we show from examples of progressively more ambitious sensor fusion systems how robots could tackle wider situations.

2. Problem Setting and Different Views at It

2.1. *Problem Setting*

The most sophisticated examples given so far like "information tracking" or "indirect search" and the recent advances outlined just above show how crucial it becomes to anticipate. There are actually two types of forecast: inner and outer. The good news with control, that is optimization mechanisms, is that whence it was implemented it can serve both. Internal optimization will cover resource management and external optimization deals with the classical task adaptation and fulfilling.

However many basic examples in the technological domain, such as memory (cache) management for instance, seem to prove that already at this level making systems more reactive does not imply making them clever. For intelligence to emerge, we conjecture that **anticipation ought to be at the same time the goal and the means to reach it!** Technically, the control requires a map to be made explicit between the situation outside – objects, interrelations, and changes – and the situation inside – modules (acquisition, processing, and decision), networks and operating –. The latter map has three major consequences:

- "Situations" imply the name "situated vision" which refers to varying, possibly dynamic, graphs at both ends;
- Situated implies a significantly more complex control than adaptive, starting from the endo/exo double nature;

- Endo/exo systems are interacting, that implies information flows between objects to be mapped on to the data-flows between modules for these flows to be controlled.

This ultimate consequence is the exact translation of the conjecture above: the map supports system control while its update is the very objective.

We can now clear the control difference between "active" and "situated" vision. The first maximizes the amount of useful information w.r.t. the task by managing resources in the system and, indirectly if no physical intervention, in the environment. The second deals with information flows inside, outside and between to maximize straight some predefined efficiency regarding a planning result.

2.2. *Different Views*

One can distinguish between four principal representations of devices running some mix of supervision and planning, each corresponding to a different scientific approach: systemic, control theory, artificial intelligence or cognitive science. Results vary according to the stress put on one or the other, and from the amount of human inspiration vs. abstract model. But as we outline briefly these four approaches, it will appear that none of them could fully support the situated vision as we are currently defining it. So we propose the intermediate type of architecture where flows between near optimal operators are controlled.

Systemic assumes any problem splits into sub-problems according to known arrangements like sequence or parallel, until complexity is low enough for the corresponding function to be designed and made by a human-size team. The difficulty comes from the atomization that generates progressively more intricate interactions between modules to still fit the initial specifications. Most of the work then tackles functional standards and protocols to reach coherent behaviors, yet quite far from intelligent ones.

Control Theory proceeds by models of the system and expected perturbations. The model embeds modules for which the state of every module contributes to the global system state. For instance actual control would rely on coordinating local state transitions. The dimension of the system (linear, complexity wise or in any meaning) soon prevents accurate modeling: sub-systems are given models augmented with degraded versions of links between states (e.g. stochastic). Approximate solutions are guaranteed enough precision or robustness margins that a targeted action or sequence of actions be completed.

Artificial Intelligence is intended here to cover the set of techniques for inference based decision making. Inference can be logical, as well as stochastic (e.g. Bayesian and derivates) or heuristic control for supervision. Each technique offers specific pros and cons triggering the designer's inventiveness to the service of complex system engineering, but still dedicated to specific limited application field (among other constraints, the so-called expertise).

Cognitive Sciences address theoretical discussions of mental representations, their nature, properties and functions. Through the idea of analogue representation, reasoning, learning and problem solving are met. Conceptual organizations provide for the so-called cognitive architectures and knowledge structuring supports some kind of generic computer implementations. The mimetic approach helps finding new theories in A.I but does not lead easily to the implementation of a given concrete application.

Back again to the orchestra,

Control theory would consider it as the owner manager does: any component comes to a fount of profit or a cause of loss to be optimized. Remember the fireman too, for whom any human or instrument is nothing but an obstacle on the others' way to escape in case of trouble etc.

Systemic behaves like the stage manager who sees instruments as boxes to ship, musicians as items to be paired in hotel rooms ...

Artificial Intelligence reminds of the conductor who exploits the real expertise respective to main task – producing music – and takes music related decisions independent of any other context

Cognitive Science would range any where between the school of music teachers or parents and the whole population of composers or musicologists, the whole set of orchestras in general or music experts.

All of them jointly provide an accurate enough view to the orchestra system, supporting its control and progress in any situation.

2.3. *Modules, Actors, Agents to Interact*

To conclude with the problem setting, let us quote here the different facets of a generic intelligent behavior that is interaction, as a working group of a dozen French teams in the fields of AI and HMI tried to represent it (see Figure 5).

The graph describes interaction mechanisms between actors of a system (agents, real processing modules etc.). It applies recursively to systems exchanging with their environment. Most branches have instances already implemented in artificial systems: information fusion, competition, planned cooperation or adaptive control. The interesting and hard point remains "opportunistic control" that covers most part of human intelligence in that much it is complementary of the rest.

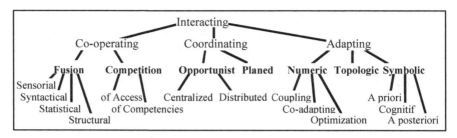

Figure 5. Taxonomy of interacting mechanisms [French Research Groups ISIS and CHM].

Computer solutions still remain to be designed and implemented. As instance, for what concerns vision, situated then, the opportunistic nature of control would translate first in Management of events changing the current situation (mainly objects appearing or disappearing in the scene) Early detection from given behaviors of selected autonomous objects. Further stages could address less specific inter object relations towards scene understanding in general.

Various types of involved complexity trigger various design approaches. Considering them all in front of the state of current design technology, it is obviously hard to spare some functional decomposition of such perception systems into communicating modules and/or layers. Some will be closer to real operation than others, but in all cases decomposing increases in turn the control problem along its two axes:

- Resource management – actuators, sensors and processors – to reach sub-goals or to focus attention
- Dimensioning of external state description and prediction (the system itself included) to anticipate what is to be expected in some suitable future.

One can consider the initial functional decomposition as a preliminary modular architecture exhibiting data flows that must be controlled in real time. The problem we try to pose well through the following examples in the next section is: "is it enough to control these flows, assuming that operator modules are well enough specified to stay between admissible error bounds and that information conveyed includes sufficient evaluation of marginal errors?"

3.   Examples of Advanced Vision Systems

3.1.   *Deliberative vs. Reactive Sensor Fusion*

Two principal axes emerged practically from robotics in the field of vision system modeling:

- the so called *deliberative* approach in which systems are not meant to deal with solving a whole problem, but they are given tools for decomposing a problem functionally into sub-problems according to predefined specialties. Then control can be operated by a planning module to systematic work-load balancing;
- the *reactive* approach in which systems complete a selection of doable moves. Examples introduced in section 1 resort to the latter family.

Most current attempts today are hybrid ones putting variable stress on "planning" or "input-output (perception-action) coupling". From section 1, Active vision appears as both a key technique in vision and obviously an intelligent process since it consists of looking for information where it is. Actually, from a control and system point of view there is no difference between sensor fusion and active vision. Both target wider system perception. The first covers an optimized cooperation between cameras and other sensors. The second covers the same between cameras and actuators. The first benefits from a priori more agile sensing and complexity is bound to resource management, the second puts image data forward and complexity is mastered through sensor control. Algorithms and techniques remain similar in both cases, so is the ultimate goal: information maximization to trigger the action right.

We thus concentrate now on sensor fusion systems. We present a few data-fusion specific architectures to exemplify the evolution of perception systems design. Such architectures can be described as hardware, system or functional. While fusion systems develop, all three complexities – practical, theoretical and functional – grow in accordance. A first attempt to master the combinatorics tied to the growing complexity is in slicing it into various functional levels. A working group sponsored by the American DOD proposed such a multi level fusion model. The six layers gather into a functional, allegedly generic, architecture model. The corresponding system descriptions are deliberative and still evolving nowadays (JDL Data Fusion Working Group [80]). Such a taxonomic (non operational) work could support task labeling and hence sub-task interoperability inside a complete system, but flows or interactions between modules are not explicit. Dasarathy [81] suggests to access data and control flows according to 3 abstraction levels: data, features, decisions. Circulating data are typified as in declarative or object-oriented programming techniques. The result is, again at the taxonomic stage, to show how rich information combining mechanisms can be. Already flows between combination-blocks are clearly identified for their semantics, and a regulation mechanism controls lower levels from partial decisions. Bedworth [82] adapts another model, the so-called OODA that is a loop crossing data-flows. The loop is closed by the action on the real world, explicitly introducing reactivity into the architecture design or control. Endsley [83] & Salerno [84] clearly belong to control theory with 4 reactive loops embedded within different functional levels of tasks. A global state controlled by a hierarchical mechanism gets preferred to data flows. It makes a mix Bedworth/Boyd and JDL approach: the major gain compared to previous models is in making the control explicit through state/communication types rather than mere data types. Bedworth and Frankel [85] go one step further in adapting some conjectures on the task management in the brain: human cognition to modeling interactions between various reasoning modalities. Two explicit flows run in opposite directions: from row data to decision and from decision to lower level control. The description shows data flows with types, circulating from one functional unit to another, but with no explicit regulation. Units are stacked according to a hierarchical abstraction principle. It thus amounts to a combination of Dasarathy and Salerno with data flows added. The human flavor enables it to bridge the different schools involved in a complex (autonomous) system design – operational, theoretic, computer –, possibly widening the class of tackled difficulties.

Although it does not always bring operative solutions out, suggesting models that make these communities work together turns out to be an efficient way of finding innovative practical solutions to new problems arising from more ambitious systems.

3.2. *JDL Data Fusion Model Extended with User Refinement*

The JDL model is a functional one obeying a strict systemic point of view. It provides a taxonomic common referential to exhibit categories of problems in the same way operational people have been thinking and organizing their systems the last decades. It currently shows five or six levels of tasks, but authors keep adding new levels making this influential model evolve [86], [87].

A stream of data (see Figure 6) enters at level 0 – the signal and image pre-processing stage to estimate and predict present objects. Then, at level 1, objects are correlated in time for tracks and identification from a priori knowledge. Most literature concentrates on these two levels.

At level 2 - situation assessment - knowledge about objects, their features and relationships is aggregated to evaluate or understand the current situation. The next level evaluates the impact of potential evolutions which the current estimated situation can turn into. Level 4 or Process Refinement supports feedback mechanisms on sensors. Related functions can then be considered part of the resource management that contributes to progressive control refinement of the data fusion. The lastly proposed level 5 - User Refinement - is an ad hoc level impersonating specific adaptations through a human interface existing in all operational systems. Note that the latter interface would be the only actual output of the system if any. "The JDL model does not speak in any detail to the notion of how the overall output of a given fusion process may be generated and controlled see [87]".

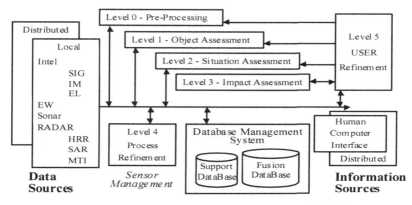

Figure 6. JDL Data Fusion Model extension proposed by Blasch [86].

Inter-level information and flow control are not fully explicit in the traditional JDL model; this is in part because the model is not an actual architecture for building fusion systems, and in part for keeping sketches simple. Note anyway that flow control would show only at level 5 and under a simple reactive form (active perception) at level 4. Inter level exchanges, represented by vertical arrows in Figure 6, are in reality protocols with attributes. On such precompiled and typified information flows one could build some flow control, yet far from truly dynamic flow control. Despite lots of papers about protocols and exact level of given functionalities, generic enough mechanisms remain to be found elsewhere [see Varshney [88] for instance].

3.3. *Data Feature Decision Model*

Unlike JDL that starts from applications, DFD grows up on tools. It takes advantage of the levels commonly agreed on in AIPR: data, feature, decision. Although taxonomic again, the work evidences a variety of fusion mechanisms to be implemented inside the very operation-level 0 of JDL. Flows - data or control - are given types or methods as in Object Oriented programming (see Figure 7). A mechanism is then represented as an arrow with acronym, such as DAI-FEO for data in/feature out (e.g. Image segmentation). Bottom up flows are natural in this scheme and horizontal flows stem from operative selection. Flow types relate to semantics, actually a generic technical scheme in these research fields, that enables regulation processes to control lower level procedures from partial decisions at upper levels, whence top-down arrows in Figure 7.

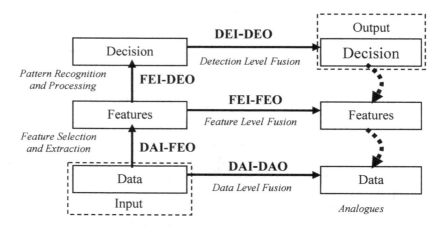

Figure 7. Data Features Decision Model by Dasarathy [81].

Such interaction mechanisms between data processing levels are extremely common in the Signal or Image Processing literature as in the Clustering or Pattern Recognition literature. They cover up to cooperative segmentation or decision loops, but they remain too elementary respective to operational considerations. Yet the representation puts forward the interest of data flow models with types and in opposite directions.

3.4. OODA Models (Cyclic Architecture)

The OODA model (see Figure 8) comes from tackling the problem: "how to make a system aware of a situation?" Technically, this is a specific question addressing a peculiar phase of perception, but it is also a universal one system wise as we proved sections 0 to 2 in struggling to better define "situated vision". Situation awareness according to Endsley [83] is the perception of the elements in the environment within a volume of time and space, the comprehension of their meaning and a projection of their status in the near future In building a so called « pilot in the loop » scenario, they underline the importance of favoring the awareness of complex, evolving situations in a jointly timely and accurate manner. On top of classical "observation, decision, action" phases of any control loop, the "orient" element is made explicit to be in charge of placing information into context. "Orient" thus appears a precursor to the decision making process, not a replacement for it [82].

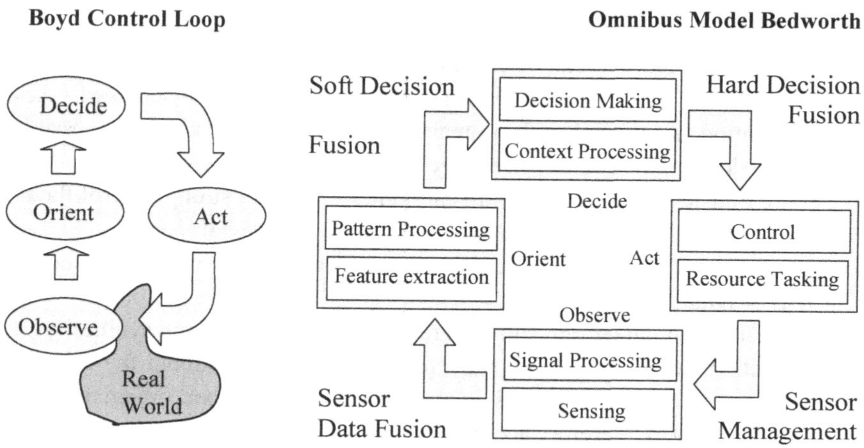

Boyd Control Loop   **Omnibus Model Bedworth**

Figure 8. Boyd's OODA model and the OMNIBUS model by Bedworth [82].

Compared to JDL and DFD, OODA adds some more system realism in closing flow loops through real world and in making action a major perception means, a truly reactive approach. Control shows up naturally as a simple mechanism in a loop. Some key technical points for the model to come to implementation are:

- The use of graphical models to express relationship between variables leading to a network.

- Whence extensive use of Bayesian networks, efficient in the case of small unidirectional graphs. However in general situations, attainable prior knowledge does not allow to construct directly a graphical model. It must be learnt [89].

- Control loop through the real world leads to time delay. Elementary versions of such control do not guaranty efficiency. For instance, developments in active vision show the importance of introducing some opportunistic orientation at each step to limit the exponential growth of local decisions.

The role of the "Orient" process is precisely to introduce an opportunistic control prior to "Decide". There, feedback aspects must be made explicit by combining system goal and task oriented projections [82]. Back to technical specificity, loops like OODA are meant to become so called processing arcs, either reflex or elaborated thinking: that implies all other control mechanisms remain to be designed explicitly, such as information fusion or action supervision on top of context handling.

3.5. *Imbricate Loop Control*

This model (see Figure 9) can be considered a generalization of the previous one where functions are included in one another rather than chained. Real implementation is targeted with as many practical considerations as possible, although it does not obey strict a reactive approach *.

Also, Endsley's description [83] is at higher level with strong control flavor. Four imbricate levels are implemented again in a single global loop:

- perception of the current situation includes most stages of models such as JDL or DFD;
- understanding the current situation requires interpretation and synthesis;
- projecting future events in a short term introduces bets about the behavior of other autonomous objects in the scene. They support imagination of possible futures, therefore acquisition or processing orientation by focusing, and eventually early detection of object-behavior changes;
- deriving a simple chain of actions from a subset of available moves requires a measure of performance, achieving the expected higher level outcome [90].

The end result is a thinking mechanism – as opposed to reflex ones – that successfully answers a 4 question flow all the way through perception ("What are the current fact?"), understanding ("What is actually going on?"), projection ("What is most likely to happen if …?") and resolution ("What exactly shall I do?"), provided a real ability to control actuators or to request and get elaboration, refinement or additional data. The questioning representation translates into protocols when thinking arcs come to implementation. Indeed, every function runs in parallel and continuous update is provided to one another in a condensed form.

It remains that such control architecture does not explicitly describe actual streams among concrete modules. For example, explicit loop termination mechanisms are needed. And following this model, even for the simplest system to run in actuality different course of actions need to compete by using a suitable performance gauge. The latter control objective, to be optimized given some application, stresses upon a necessarily wider conceptual frame to embed states in.

---

* The approach becomes reactive when control, e.g. loop ending, depends on contextual information bound to instant objectives revised according to, for the moment, pre compiled schemes.

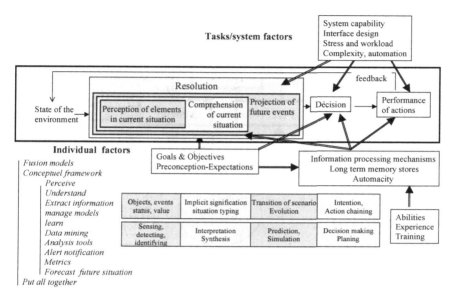

Figure 9. Endsley [83] and McGuinnes extension [90] model.

3.6. *Human Conceptualization: Architecture with Two Streams*

Frankel & Bedworth [85] endeavor to translate a more elaborate concept of controlled global expectation allegedly a key one in human thinking. The result is a mix of the respectively chained and inclusive models in 4) and 5). Working by graph descriptions, Frankel [85] elaborates an architecture (Figure 10-a) with two self-regulatory processes: local (from stimuli to response) according to time response or goal focalization and global/emotional (from expectation to perception) to govern goal setting and adaptive control. One gets two antagonists flows with types and various control flows. The first stream is classical in other fusion models. The second operates backwards: bets are made on the dynamics of autonomous objects discovered in the scene and possible futures are analyzed. That supports prediction to control goals of the local loop by re-orienting the perception and re-organizing sub-goals. Some other important streams exist to tighten the coupling between local and global loops.

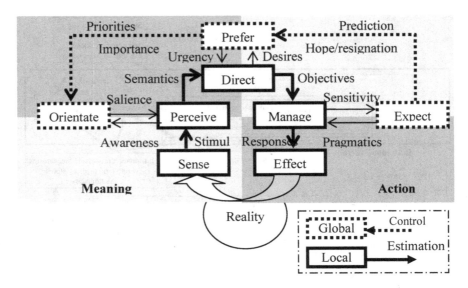

Figure 10-a. Frankel's [85] humanoid model.

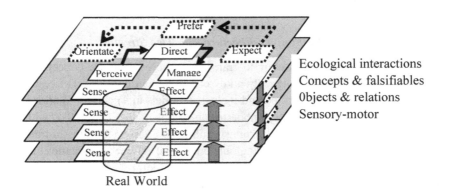

Figure 10-b. Frankel's [85] abstract levels.

For implementing again different levels of a perceptive hierarchy (Figure 10-b), the same graph is duplicated and superposed with a mechanism of inter-level communication. Two coupling exist then: one in parallel (at every level) through the real world, the other serial following the inter-level mechanism. A major draw-back of this model is its growing complexity with generality, up to a point where actual activity control becomes beyond technical ability. No explicit regulation mechanism is provided; they would probably vary significantly with different applicative instances. A hierarchy of four abstraction levels is probably realistic enough according to different known classes of human reasoning. But duplicating a same model at all levels together with implementing simplified interactions does not facilitate the overall control.

3.7. *Conclusion: Building Blocks vs. Architecture*

Examples confirm that evolution centers ultimately on information flows. Indeed, the two first examples are progressively closer to operational, their component operators are progressively better identified for control and system states get better defined. JDL concentrates on tactical functionalities bound to the real operations world; DFD is more concerned with practical vision implementation. The three last ones regress somehow in that operators would become too much detailed respective to the goal. In concentrating on data and control flows, they offer processing arcs to support fusion mechanisms at various semantic levels.

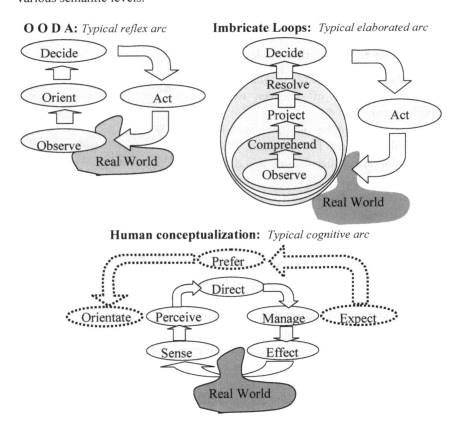

Figure 11. Embedding processing arcs in suitable schemes.

However, that makes it difficult then to compute inference mechanisms. But also we noticed that they translate different concerns in reusing similar basic blocks and associating them differently (Figure 11). OODA as a flat loop fits reflex processes. To support more elaborate reasoning with competing predictive solutions the second type embeds similar functions into nested loops. The last one takes after them in exhibiting one more flow, actually a distributed supervision, in the opposite way through similar functions again. All three can use stacks of such loops, each devoted to a given semantic level.

So, at some point between the second and third examples, the combinatorics of interactions appears worth the control. Eventually, system design comes back again to the control of communications between modules which are supposed

1- *to have been locally tailored to their individual task*
2- to be in a situation of completing the task in known (preferably optimal) conditions.

Then, neither do they need to be described with too many details anymore, nor do they require frequent control.

4. Conclusion: Yet Another Model?

Eventually it appeared that best solutions would come from a trade off between two quite opposite trends:

- integrating modular sub-functions within a global and general fusion system,
- chaining active mechanisms in a dedicated application.

Figure 12: an application of autonomous vehicle guidance.

The frontier between the two kinds of design schemes tends to become fuzzy, as and when versatile reactions or intricate timeliness-accuracy-and-scope reactions are necessary to the application of autonomous vehicle guidance (Figure 12). Our own model (Figure 13) intends to be general enough so that it could instantiate any previous model outlined above depending on the class of situation and on the application. At the same time it is implemented right upon design onto an autonomous car.

The primary interaction with the exo-system is made of the so-called processing arcs (bottom right). They were designed elsewhere (classical algorithms, usual hardware devices, culturally agreed functions, bio-inspired etc.). Each one supports some nominal functioning in active or reactive perception and was proved an efficient mechanism in a given set of contexts*. They are inserted here in a pure OODA style where the loop closes through the centralized control chain - 1 to 5 - on the left. In most cases several steps will be by-passed, like 2 and 4 in a positive pedestrian detection, to get faster reaction. Note that this will change the state of the currently active arcs as well. As many arcs as necessary can be implemented and concurrently run in a preventive way: for the time being and sake of actual operationallity referring to the car, arcs are sorted by the amount of perceptive wondering and thus action delay.

Control is achieved by a centralized module (left) under the form of a column of five moves:

1- Update the scene-knowledge
2- Select possible behaviors to compete
3- Re-define short to mid-term objectives
4- Plan actions
5- Trigger actions

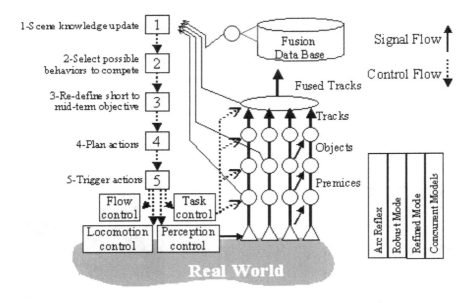

Figure 13. Instantiating a double flow towards opportunist control.

---

* Let us underline that this is an exact translation of the postulate proposed with the orchestra metaphor.

Such procedural steps are quite common (see TEA1 for instance), the novelty here if any resides in key step number 3. Control at that stage concentrates on three variables supporting anticipation: term (time), field (space) and imagination (data base). Each one is sampled into three values "short, medium and long". That makes our architectural translation of the situated vision concept (see 1.3 and conclusion of 2.1) generalizing the active vision concept: for instance steps 2 and 4 enable prediction that is a major difference between active and situated, without disturbing reflexes that ignore them. For instance, assuming a wider objective as for a car "stick to the road", looking for a target where it will be rather than where it is requires:

- step 2 to select potential behaviours from fused tracks and local models out of the data base,
- step 3 to decide upon anticipation and then "filter" on "important" behaviours w.r.t. programmed objectives, and translate the latter behaviours into intermediate requests
- step 4 to compile the requests into the language of available modules sensors and tools
- step 5 to trigger adequate facilities in right conditions (timely, accurately, energy wise).

Eventually, to act these steps, the central control module monitors four entities: perception (active vision), locomotion (robotics, vehicle), control and supervision (of tasks to be implemented on data flows of processing arcs), and last but not least flow control. Two are resources to be managed and two are means to be controlled. The whole structure gets activated upon events output by processing arcs or by tasks continuously running on the Fusion Data Base.

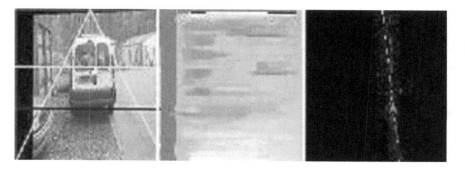

Figure 14. Examples of vision results (from left to right: obstacle with superimposed perspective indexes, disparity map, dot alignment towards trajectory (from the 3D predictive guess)).

Other instances of the proposed model are doable but the present one, implementing an event-triggered central control, creates a suitable test bed for experimenting on both simplifying views to human intelligence as promoted by cognitive sciences and architectural concerns to enable external intelligent behavior. That way, a versatile architecture model is put to a concrete form by trading off between structured sets of application driven high level functionalities, too much general to reach operability, and operative flow driven constructs without enough organisation variability to be representative of true system intelligence. This architecture kernel is intended to accept continuously changing objectives which would carry out bases of situated vision.

References

1. E.D. Dickmans, Simulation for the development of a visual autopilot-system for road vehicles, *Automotive Simulation*, M.R. Heller (ed.), Springer-Verlag, 1989, pp. 11-22.
2. B. Myslivetz, E.D. Dickmans, Recursive 3D road and relative ego-state recognition, *IEEE Trans. PAMI*, spec. issue on Interpretation of 3D scenes, Feb. 1992.
3. E.D. Dickmans, V. Graefe, Dynamic monocular machine vision and applications, *Jour. of Machine vision and application*, Springer int., Nov. 1988, pp.223-261.
4. E.D. Dickmans, 4-D Dynamic vision for intelligent motion control, *Int: Jour. for Engineering Applications of A.I.*, spec. issue on Autonomous Intelligent Vehicles, C. Harris (ed.),1991.
5. E.D. Dickmanns, Expectation-based dynamic scene understanding, *Active Vision*, MIT Press, 1992, pp. 303-335.
6. E.D. Dickmanns, B. Mysliwetz, and T. Christians, An integrated spatio-temporal approach to automatic visual guidance of autonomous vehicles, *IEEE Transactions on Systems, Man and Cybernetics*, 20(6), Nov. 1990, pp. 1273-1284.
7. M. Hebert. 3-D Landmark Recognition from Range Images, *IEEE Conference on Computer Vision and Pattern Recognition*, Champaign, June 1992, pp. 360-365.
8. I.S. Kweon, T. Kanade. High Resolution Terrain Map from Multiple Data., *IEEE International Workshop on Intelligent Robots and Systems*, Tsuchiura, Jul. 1990.
9. I. S. Kweon, Modeling Rugged Terrain by Mobile Robots with Multiple Sensors. *Ph.D. thesis, Robotics Institute, Carnegie Mellon University*, Feb. 1991.
10. M. Daily, J. Harris, D. Keirsey, K. Olin, D. Payton, K. Reiser, J. Rosenblatt, D. Tseng' V. Wong. Autonomous Cross-Country Navigation with the ALV, *IEEE Int. Conf. on Robotics and Automation*, Philadelphia, pp.718-726, Apr.1988.

11. R.A. Brooks, R. Greiner, T.O. Binford, The ACRONYM model-based vision system., *6th International Joint Conference on Artificial Intelligence,* Tokyo, Aug. 1979, pp. 105-113.
12. R.A. Brooks. Symbolic Reasoning among 3D Models and 2D Images. *Artificial Intelligence,* vol. 17, pp. 285-348, 1981.
13. T.O. Binford, Visual perception by a computer, *IEEE conf. on Systems and Control,* Miami, Dec 1971.
14. R.A. Brooks, T.O. Binford, Representing and reasoning about specified scenes, *Proc. DARPA IU workshop,* Apr. 1980, pp. 95-103.
15. G. Giralt, R. Chatila, R. Alami,. Remote Intervention, Robot Autonomy, and Teleprogramming: Generic Concepts and Real-World Application Cases, *IEEE Int. Workshop on Intelligent Robots and Systems,* Yokohama (Japan), Juillet 1993,pp. 314-320.
16. G. Giralt, L. Boissier, The French Planetary Rover Vap: Concept and Current Developments, *IEEE International Workshop on Intelligent Robots and Systems,* Raleigh, Jul. 1992, pp. 1391-1398.
17. R. Chatila. *L'expérience du robot mobile HILARE.Tech. Rep. n°. 3188,* Laboratoire d'Automatique et d'Analyse des Systèmes (C.N.R.S.), Toulouse (France),1984.
18. P. Fillatreau, M. Devy, Localization of an Autonomous Mobile Robot from 3D Depth Images using heterogeneous Feature, *IEEE International Workshop on Intelligent Robots and Systems,* Yokohama (Japan), Jul. 1993.
19. P. Grandjean, A. Robert de Saint- Vincent, 3-D modeling of indoor scenes by fusion of noisy range and stereo data, *IEEE International Conference on Robotics and Automation,* Scottsdale, May 1989, pp. 681-687.
20. M. Devy, J. Colly, P. Grandjean, T. Baron, Environment Modelling from a Laser / Camera Multisensor System., *IARP 2nd Workshop on Multi-Sensor Fusion and Environment Modelling,* Oxford (U.K.), Sept. 1991.
21. F. Nashashibi, Ph. Fillatreau, B. Dacre-Wright, T. Simeon. 3D Autonomous Navigation in a Natural Environment, *IEEE International Conference on Robotics and Automation,* San Diego, May 1994.
22. P. Moutarlier, P. Grandjean, R. Chatila. Multisensory Data Fusion for Mobile Robot Location and 3D Modeling, *IARP 1st Workshop on Multi-Sensor Fusion and Environment Modeling,* Toulouse (France), Oct. 1989.
23. S. Lacroix, P. Fillatreau, F. Nashashibi, R. Chatila, M. Devy, Perception for Autonomous Navigation in a Natural Environment, *Workshop on Computer Vision for Space Applications,* Antibes (France), Sept. 1993.
24. J. Aloimonos, I. Weiss, A. Bandopadhay, Active vision, *International Journal of Computer Vision,* 1(4) pp. 333-356, 1987.
25. R. Bajcsy. Active perception vs. passive perception, *Proceedings of the IEEE,* 1985, pp. 55-59.
26. V. Anantharam, P. Varaiya, Optimal strategy for a conflict resolution problem. *System and Control Letters,* 1986.

27. B. Zavidovique, A. Lanusse, P. Garda, Robot perception systems: some design issues, *NATO Adv. Res. Work. MARATEA*, A.K. Jain Ed. Springer Verlag, Aug. 87.
28. X. Merlo, Techniques probabilistes d'intégration et de contrôle de la perception en vue de son exploitation par le système de décision d'un robot, *PhD. thesis*, Institut National Polytechnique de Lorraine, France, 1988.
29. Y. Aloimonos, Visual shape computation, *Proc. of the IEEE,* 76(8), jan. 1988, pp. 899-916.
30. C. Fermüller, Y. Aloimonos. Vision and action, *Image and vision computing.* 13(10), Dec. 1993, pp.725-744.
31. P. Boukir. *"Reconstruction 3D d'un environnement statique par vision active"*, PhD thesis, Oct. 1993.
32. F. Chaumette, S. Boukir, P. Bouthemy, D. Juvin, Structure from controlled motion, *IEEE Transactions on PAMI,* 4(11), Feb. 1996, pp.372-389.
33. X. Merlo, A. Lanusse, B. Zavidovique, Optimal control of a robot perception system, *IASTED Int'l Symp. GENEVE,* 1987.
34. B.Zavidovique, Perception for decision or Decision for perception? *Human and Machine Perception,* V. Cantoni Ed. Plenum Press, 1997, pp. 155-178.
35. R. Bajczy, Active perception, 8(76), aug. 1988, pp. 996-1005.
36. J. Maver and R. Bajcsy. Occlusion as a guide for planning the next view, *IEEE Trans. on Pattern Analysis and Machine intelligence,* 15(5), May 1993, pp 417-433.
37. R. Pito, A sensor based solution to the next best view problem, *IAPR Int. Conf on Pattern Recognition,* Aug. 1996, pp. 941-945.
38. J. Koseka, H. Christensen, and R. Bajcsy, Discrete event modeling of visually guided behaviors, *International Journal of Computer Vision,* 14(2), Mai 1995, pp.179-191.
39. P. Whaite and F. Ferrie. Autonomous exploration: Driven by uncertainty,. *IEEE International conference on Computer Vision and Pattern Recognition, CVPR '94,* Seattle, pp. 339-346, June 1994.
40. D.H. Ballard, Animate vision, *Artificial Intelligence,* 48(1), Août 1991, pp.57-86.
41. D. Noton, L. Stark, Eye movement and visual perception, *Scientific American,* 224(6), Juin 1971, pp. 34-43.
42. A.L. Yarbus, Eye movements and vision,. *Plenum Press,* 1967.
43. E. Milios, M. Jenkin, and J. Tsotsos, Design and performance of trish, a binocular robot head with torsional eye movements, *International Journal of Pattern Recognition and Artificial Intelligence,* 7(1), Février 1993, pp. 51-68.
44. D. Murray, K. Bradshaw, P. McLauchlan, P. Sharkey, Driving saccade to pursuit using image motion, *International Journal of Computer Vision,* 16(3), Mars 1995, pp. 205-228.
45. J. Tsosos, A complexity level analysis of vision, *IEEE Int. Conf on Computer Vision, ICCV'87,* London, June 1987.

46. K. Brunnstrom, J.O. Eklundh, and T. Uhlin, Active fixation for scene exploration, *International Journal of Computer Vision,* 17(2), Feb. 1996, pp.137-162.
47. Y. Aloimonos, Purposive and qualitative active vision, *IAPR Conf. on Pattern Recognition ICPR '90,* Atlantic City, pp.346-360.
48. M.I. Tarr, M.J. Black, A computational and evolutionary perspective on the role of representation in vision,. *Computer Vision, Graphics, and Image Processing: Image Unedrstanding,* jul. 1994, pp. 65-73.
49. C. Brown, Towards general vision, *Computer Vision, Graphics, and Image Processing: Image Understanding,* 60(1), 1994, pp.89-91.
50. S. Sandini, E. Grosso, Why purposive vision? *Computer Vision Graphics, and Image Processing: Image Understanding,* 60(1), 1994, pp. 109-112.
51. A. L. Abbott and N. Ahuja. Active surface reconstruction by integrating focus, vergence, stereo and camera calibration, *Third International Conference on Computer Vision,* 1990, pp. 489-492.
52. B. B. Bederson, R. S. Wallace, E. L. Schwartz, Two miniature pan-tilt devices, *International Conference on Robotics and Automation,* 1992, pp. 658-663.
53. C. Brown, Gaze controls cooperating through prediction, *Image and vision computing,*8(1), 1990, pp. 10-17.
54. C.M. Brown, Kinematic and 3D motion prediction for gaze control, *Wrkshop on Interpretation of 3D Scenes,* 1989, pp.145-151.
55. W.S. Ching, P.S. Toh, K.L. Chan, M.H. Er, Robust vergence with concurrent detection of occlusion and specular highlights, *Fourth Int. Conference on Computer Vision,* 1993, pp. 384-394.
56. J.J. Clark, N.J. Ferrier, Modal control of an attentive vision system, *2nd Int. Conf. on Computer Vision,* 1988, pp. 514-523.
57. D. Coombs, C. Brown, Real-time smooth pursuit tracking for a moving binocular robot, *Computer Vision and Pattern Recognition,* 1992, pp.23-28.
58. J. L. Crowley, P. Bobet, M. Mesrabi, Gaze control for a binocular camera head, *2nd European Conf. on Computer Vision,* 1992, pp. 588-596.
59. J. C. Fiala, R. Lumia, K. J. Roberts, A. J. Wavering, Triclops: a tool for studying active vision, *International Journal of Computer Vision,* 12(2, 3), 1994, pp.231-250.
60. E. Grosso, D. H. Ballard, Head-centered orientation strategies in animate vision, *4th Int. Conf. on Computer Vision,* pp. 395-402.
61. I. Horswill and M. Yamamoto, A $ 1000 active stereo vision system, CVPR94.
62. E. Krotkov, F. Fuma, J. Summers, An agile stereo camera system for flexible image acquisition, *IEEE Journal on Robotics and Automation,* 4(1), 1988, pp.108-113.
63. B. Marsh, C. Brown, T. LeBlanc, M. Scott, T. Becker, P. Das, J. Karlsson, C. Quiroz, Operating system support for animate vision. *Jour. of Parallel and Distributed Computing,* 15, 1992, pp.103-117.

64. D.W. Murray, P.F. McLauchlan, I.D. Reid, and P.M. Sharkey, Reactions to peripheral image motion using a head/eye platform, *4th International Conference on Computer Vision*, 1993, pp 403-411.

65. K. Pahlavan, J. O. Eklundh, A head-eye system-analysis and design, *Computer Vision, Graphics, and Image Processing: Image Understanding*, 56(1), Jul. 1992, pp.41-56.

66. K. Pahlavan, T. Uhlin, and J.O. Eklundh, Integrating primary ocular processes, 2nd European Conference on Computer Vision, May 1992, pp 526-541.

67. K. Pahlavan, T. Uhlin, and J.O. Eklundh, Dynamic fixation, *4th Int. Conf. on Computer Vision*, May 1993, pp. 412-419.

68. K.N.Kutulakos, C.R. Dyer, Recovering shape by purposive view-point adjustment, *Computer Vision and Pattern Recognition*, June 1992, pp.16-22.

69. K.N. Kutulakos, C.R. Dyer, Recovering shape by purposive viewpoint adjustment, *International Journal of Computer Vision*, 12(2/3), 1992, pp.113-136.

70. R. Pissard-Gibollet, P. Rives, Asservissement visuel appliqué à un robot mobile: Etat de l'art et modélisation cinématique. *Research report RR1577*, INRIA-Sophia Antipolis, France, Dec. 1991.

71. L. E. Wixson, Exploiting world structure to efficiently search for objects, *Technical Repport 434*, University of Rochester, C. S. Department, Rochester, New York, Jul. 1992.

72. L. E. Wixson, Gaze selection for visual search, *PhD thesis, University of Rochester*, Rochester, New York, 1994.

73. L. Birnbaum, M. Brand, and P. Cooper, Looking for trouble: using causal semantics to direct focus of attention, *4th International Conference on Computer Vision*, May 1993, pp. 49-56.

74. R. D. Rimey P. A. von Kaenel, C. M. Brown, Goal-oriented dynamic vision, *Technical report, University of Rochester*, New York, Aug. 1993.

75. R. D. Rimey. Control of selective perception using Bayes nets and decision theory, *PhD thesis, University of Rochester*, New York, Dec 1993.

76. M. Isard, A. Blake. Contour tracking by stochastic propagation of conditional density, *European Conf. on Computer Vision*, Cambridge 1996, pp. 343-356.

77. M. Isard, A. Blake. CONDENSATION: unifying low-level and high-level tracking in a stochastic framework, *5th European conference on Computer Vision*, 1998.

78. O. Dessoude, Contrôle Perceptif en milieu hostile: allocation de ressources automatique pour un système multicapteur, *PhD Thesis*, University Paris-Sud, 1993.

79. C. Olivier, Stratégies d'acquisition, de traitement et de prise en compte d'informations pour contrôle de robot en environnement non structuré. *PhD. thesis*, University Paris-Sud, 1993.

80. A. Steinberg, C. Bowman, F. White, 'Revision to the JDL Data fusion Model'. *Proc. of AeroSense Conference, SPIE* vol. 3719, pp. 430,441, 1999.
81. B. Dasarathy, "Optimal Features-In Feature-Out (FEIFEO) Fusion for Decisions in Multisensor Environments", *Proc. SPIE 3376, Sensor Fusion: Architectures, Algorithms and Applications II,* 1998.
82. M. Bedworth, J. O'Brien, 'The Omnibus Model: A New Model for Data Fusion?' *Proc. of FUSION'99, Sunyvale,* USA, 1999.
83. M. Endsley, 'Towards a Theory of Situation Awareness in Dynamic Systems'. *Human Factors Journal,* vol. 37, pp. 32-64, 1995.
84. J. Salerno, 'Information Fusion: a High-Level Architecture Overview', *Proc. of FUSION'00,* Paris, 2000.
85. C.B. Frankel, M. Bedworth, 'Control, Estimation and Abstraction in Fusion Architectures: Lessons from Human Information Processing'. *Proc. of FUSION'00,* Paris, 2000.
86. J. Gainey, E. Blasch, 'Development of Emergent Processing Loops as a System of Systems Concept'. *Proc. of AeroSense Conference, SPIE* vol 3179, pp 186-195, 1999.
87. J. Llinas, C. Bowman, G. Rogova, A. Steinberg, E. Waltz, F. White, 'Revisions and Extensions to the JDL Data Fusion Model II', *Proc. of FUSION'04,* Stockolm, 2004.
88. P.K. Varshney, Distributed detection and data fusion, *Springer ed.,* NewYork, 1997.
89. P. Bladon, R. Hall & A. Wright, 'Situation assessment using graphical models', *Proc. of FUSION'02,* Toronto, 2002.
90. B. McGuinness, J. Foy, 'A subjective measure of situation awareness: the Crew Awareness Rating Scale (CARS)', *Proc of the first Human Peformance Situation awarenes, and automation conference,* Savannah, Georgia, 2000.

RECOGNIZING OCCLUDED FACE USING FRACTALS

ANDREA F. ABATE, MICHELE NAPPI, DANIEL RICCIO, MAURIZIO TUCCI

Dipartimento di Matematica e Informatica, Università di Salerno,
Fisciano, Salerno 84084, Italy

A lot of importance has been given to the security problems in the last years. Particularly, secure access in reserved area with consentient people. Face Recognition works well providing high recognition rate with consentient/non-consentient people. However we have to deal with occlusions, such as sunglasses or scarfs. In this chapter a new face recognition method, namely ROF, is proposed, it is based on IFS (Iterated Function Systems) theory, in which the information used for the indexing and recognition task is made local, in order to render the method robust with respect to possible occlusions. The distribution of similarities in the face image is exploited as a signature for the identity of the subject. Besides it has been investigated on the amount of informations provided by each component of the face, first independently and then all together.

1. Introduction

In last years security problems are capturing most of the attention of the researchers. Particularly the people authentication problem. There are many situation, in which the authentication problem is crucial, such as limited access to reserved areas, check in, banking. The most commonly used approaches consist in login and password, badges and cards. However login or password can be forgotten, while cards and badges can be stolen or counterfeit. All these drawbacks can be avoided if it succeeds in binding people identity to its anatomical characteristics, which have to possess the following properties: Universality, Distinctiveness, Permanence, Collectability. This kind of metric is referred as biometric, from *bio* = life and *metric* = measure. A lot of anatomical features, such as fingerprint, hand-shape or iris have been studied until today. For each of them a wide study has been made, in order to assure the properties stated before. It is observed that two main characteristics enact the success of a biometry: reliability and people acceptance. Indeed, iris recognition represents the most reliable approach, but it is too much intrusive. On the contrary, fingerprint are easily applicable, but it cannot be used with non consentient people. As very nice compromise between acceptance and reliability, face recognition is emerging. Recognition rate of face biometric cannot be compared to that of iris and fingerprint. However the ease in snapshot and video capturing make this method effective also when the subject does not collaborate or he ignores to be recognized. Research has been made attempting to make face recognition systems fully automatic and searching for successful classifiers for face features. Existing approaches for Face Recognition can be classified in three principal cathegories, as suggested by Zhao *et al.* [6]: ***Holistic methods*** - Eigenfaces, Fisherfaces, Support Vector Machine, Independent Component Analysis, ***Feature-based methods*** - Dynamic Link Architecture, Hidden Markov Model, Convolution Neural Networks and ***Hybrid methods*** - Modular eigenfaces, Component-based. All these methods deal with a large set of typical drawbacks in face recognition, such as variation in expression, lighting, pose and acquisition time. None of these techniques is free from limitations. Furthermore there exist few works and investigations about the problem of the occlusions, such as Martinez [2], based on probabilistic approaches or neural networks. The main contribution of this chapter is then the application of fractal based technique, solving the face recognition problem in presence of synthetic and natural occlusions, such as rectangular occlusion or sunglasses and scarfs. The new proposed strategy applies IFS (Iterated Function Systems), largely used in image compression and indexing [1] & [5]. The affine transformations are used in order to characterize auto-similarities into a face image, extracting a compact feature vector with high discriminant power. The rest of this chapter is organized as follows. Section 2.   shows in more detail the feature extraction process. Furthermore in Section 3.   a new distance function is provided in order to make comparisons among models computed for the input face images and in Section 4.   a concise description of the measures and databases used during tests is given in order to make clear presented results. At last the conclusions are drawn in Section 5.   .

2. Feature Extraction

As said in Section 1.   many approaches address the problem of face recognition also under different light conditions or in presence of meaningful variations in expression, but few of them work well when face images are partial occluded by accessories, such as sunglasses or scarfs. The face recognition method presented in this chapter also deals with partial occlusions. In order to render this method robust with respect to probably occlusions the features extraction process is made local to the interesting region, defining four main areas, which are: left eye, right eye, nose and mouth, as shown in Figure 1 (a). For each of these regions a set of fiducial point is extract and the average approximation error is computed, so that point locations and approximation errors represent the signature for the face.

The first problem to be solved is the face localization. Indeed the face region has to be extracted from the input face image. To select manually position for those elements results in a more precise localization and better performances in terms of accuracy of the system. Then in this case with a semi-automatic application the center of the eyes and baseline of the nose are manually selected, extracting a face region proportional to the distance among these three points.

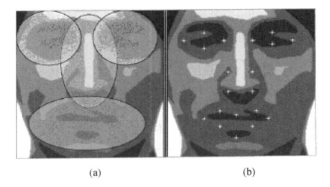

(a)   (b)

Figure 1. Region of interest (a) and location of the entry points (b) on the face image.

At last the face region extracted from the input image is normalized to a 256×256 dimension, while nothing has been done for the original warping of the input images, which also can affect the performances of the method in terms of recognition rate.

The second problem consists in computing the signature for the extracted face image, then the process of computing centroids is now explained in more details, particularly the way in which the IFS have been re-handled in order to localize the features and organize them in a compact signature for the face image. The face objects are independently indexed by means of the IFS systems as separate regions of interest. For each region of interest (eyes, nose or mouth) a set of fixed points $P=\{P_1, P_2, ..., P_n\}$, called *entry points* is considered. The position of the entry points has been fixed in advance in our case, but it is also possible to locate dynamically the face objects in the input image with a fully automatic method, then refining more accurately the position of the set of points P. For each $P_i=(x_i, y_i) \in P$, ROF extracts the corresponding range $R_{xi,yi}$, whose upper-left corner falls in the position P_i. It searches for the first n best fitting domains with respect to an affine transformation. In order to render the method more robust with respect to small shifts around the entry position (x_i, y_i) 18 nearest neighbors of the current entry points are considered. In order to make useful the informations about the distribution of similarities brought out during the indexing phase, the range/domain relations have to be organized in a linear vector, so that comparisons will be possible in the next. In this case domains are organized in a set of clusters $C=\{C_1, C_2, ..., C_m\}$, each of them represented by its centroid c_i, while centroids are stored in memory as a list. Each centroid in the list stores its spatial coordinates computed as the mean of the coordinates of the domains belonging to the cluster and also the average approximation error between domains and the prefixed block:

$$C_x = \frac{\sum\limits_{D \in C} D_x}{|C|}, \quad Cy = \frac{\sum\limits_{D \in C} D_y}{|C|}$$

(1)

$$C_{err} = \frac{\sum\limits_{D \in C} \sqrt{\sum\limits_{i=1}^{|PB|} \left(PB(i) - \left(\alpha \cdot D(i) - \beta\right)\right)^2}}{|C|}$$

At first the list of centroids is empty. Starting from the first entry point, the corresponding range is extracted and n best fitting domains are searched. The domains are clusterized one at a time. Initially the list of centroids is empty, then a new cluster is created, for the first domain and its centroid has the same coordinates of the inserted domain. The second domain fitting the current range is then extracted by means of the IFS transformation and it has to be inserted in the correct cluster. ROF scans the list of centroids searching for the centroid with minimum distance. If no cluster is found a new cluster is created for the domain and added to the list, while the corresponding centroid has the same coordinates and approximation error of the inserted domain. On the contrary, if there is a cluster, whose centroid is not more far than a fixed threshold ε from the domain to be inserted, ROF tries to update the cluster with the new domain. The new coordinates are computed for the centroid according to Eq. (1) but taking account also of the new domain. It is checked if after the update operation of the coordinates there exists a domain in the cluster, whose distance from the recomputed centroid is greater than the fixed threshold ε. In this case the updating operation fails and a new cluster is created having the same coordinates and approximation error of the inserted domain.

In Figure 2 a graphical representation of the updating process is reported. The domain D_1 has to be inserted and the list of centroids is empty, then the cluster C_1 is created with centroid c_1. Subsequently in order to insert the domain D_2, ROF searches for the nearest centroid in the whole list, in this case only c_1. Supposing that c_1 results to be the nearest centroid, ROF computes the new coordinates as the mean of the coordinates of c_1 and D_2, testing whether the

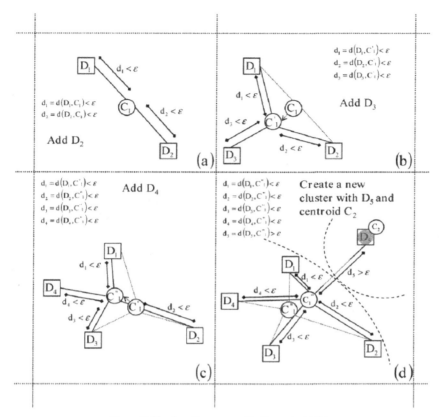

Figure 2. The insertion process for the centroid list.

distance among the domains in the cluster and the new centroid position are still smaller of the maximum allowed distance ε, which represents the radius of the cluster. If the test succeeds the domain D_2 is added to the cluster, the centroid position and the approximation error are updated as suggested by the Equations (1) with the situation in Figure 2 (a). This operation is repeated for next domains D_3 and D_4, Figure 2 (b) and (c).

At last, supposing the test for domain D_5 fails because during the update of the centroid position for c_1 there will be domains in the corresponding cluster with distance greater than ε, that represents the maximum radius for a cluster. In this case a new cluster is created with centroid c_2 located at the coordinates of its domain $D5$, Figure 2 (d). In the same way if any centroid is found for a domain, in scanning the list of centroids, a new cluster is created. At last, in order to deal with small shifts of the eyes, nose and mouth in the extracted face region due to the errors committed during the feature localization process, also a limited number of nearest neighbor of the original ranges corresponding to the entry points are considered. Starting from the current entry point all centroids are computed by means of the aforesaid algorithm, then with a spiral visit centered in the current entry point height neighbor of the range are considered. These neighbors are kept on an Archimede's spiral $\rho = a \cdot \theta$ where ρ is the distance from the center to the tracing point, θ is the angular distance covered and a is a fixed constant. With the spiral visit, higher the distance from the entry point minor the considered number of neighbors. This makes sense if it is taken in account that more far the neighbor from the current entry point, minor their similarity with the current range. Then avoiding the problem of small shifts the probability that the correct entry point falls near to the prefixed position is higher. Once the list of centroids has been computed, it has to be rearranged so that a distance function can be defined for the next comparisons. It is sensible that, comparing two face images the approximation error of a centroid belonging to former with the error of the nearest centroid in the latter is matched. However this makes the comparison task much expensive. Indeed each centroid in the list of centroids consists of two coordinates $C(x,y)$, the nearness of two centroids can be esteemed by the euclidean norm. Let be L_1 a list of centroids with length $n=|L_1|$ to be compared with another L_2, with length $m=|L_2|$. For each centroid $C^k_{L_1}$ in L_1 the nearest centroid $C^j_{L_2}$ in L_2 is searched and the absolute difference between the correspondent approximation errors $|e^k_{C_{L_1}} - e^j_{C_{L_2}}|$ is computed. The computational cost of this operation is so $O(n \cdot m)$. Of course it can be done better, if the centroids in the list L_1 are organized in a KD-Tree spending $O(n\log(n))$, in $\log(m)$ time the searched centroid $C^j_{L_i}$ is retrieved, then the overall computational cost reduces to $O(n\log(n)+n\log(m)) = O(n\log(n \cdot m))$. Now it can be tried to obtain a better result representing spatial location of centroids with the Peano keys. Given a centroid $C(x,y)$, the correspondent Peano key a_C is computed interleaving bits of x and y, from the less significant digit to the most one. From the literature it is known that Peano keys are useful in indexing tasks because mapping a 2D space in a 1D space, they preserve most of the spatial information of the original data. In the next step the computed keys are sorted, this can be done in a linear time $O(n)$ with the Radix Sort algorithm. Making comparison between L_1 and L_2, $O(m)$ time is spent in order to search for the centroid $C^j_{L_2}$ in L_2 nearest to the first centroid $C^1_{L_1}$ in L_1, holding memory of j_1. Then it is observed that, generally, the location of the next centroid in L_2 nearest to a centroid $C^k_{L_1}$ falls not so far from the position j_k, about j_k+c, where experimentally c has been found as about $0 \le c \le 10$ and j_k is the location in L_2 of the nearest of $C^{k-1}{}_{L_1}$ in L_1, with $k>1$. Then for each centroids in L_1 it has to be tested only c centroids in L_2, so that the overall complexity of the comparisons is now $O(n+c \cdot m) = O(n+m)$ that is linear because c is a constant. Having a low computational complexity making comparisons is crucial considering that in a huge database of face images, millions of images could have to be tested. Now the Peano curve rearrangement of the centroids and its consequent advantages are shortly examined. Let be L a list of centroids. Each centroid in L hold two main informations, that are the centroid coordinates $C(x,y)$ and the approximation error e_{C_L} of the domains in the correspondent cluster. ROF generates the Peano key for each centroid in L, interleaving the bits of x and y. Sorting these keys in a new list L^* according to the Peano curve there are two main advantages. In the first instance the distance between two feature vectors can be computed efficiently as described above. Second the information is organized in a one dimensional array, localizing eyes, nose and mouth in a fixed location. This is useful when a subject has to be authenticate only by means a subset of its facial features. Furthermore in this way, partial occlusion in the face image can be easily located.

3. Definition of the Distance Function $\Delta(A, B)$

In this section the distance function used comparing two different face features vector is defined. The dominion of this function consists of bi-dimensional vectors $S \in R^2$ where $(a,b) \in S$ with a a Peano key and b a real value representing the mean value of the approximation error for the centroid centered in $a = P(x,y)$. Given two vectors $S,T \in R^2$ the operator $\psi(S,T)$ is defined as follows:

$$\psi_i(S,T) = \left| b_T^{\mu(S,T)} - b_S^i \right| \qquad (2)$$

with

$$\mu(S,T) = \min_j \left\| a_T^j - a_S^i \right\|$$

that is $\mu(S,T)$ represents the index in T of the point $a_T^i = P_1(x_1,y_1)$ nearest to the point $a_S^i = P_2(x_2,y_2)$ in S.

Then for each item $a_s = P_s(x,y) \in S$ it is search for the nearest item $a_T = P_T(x,y) \in T$ according to the euclidean norm $\|P_S - P_T\|_2$ and the quantity $|b_S - b_T|$ is computed, that is the absolute difference of the approximation errors corresponding to the nearest points $P_s \in S$ and $P_T \in T$. At last summation on i of the values of $\psi_i(S,T)$ is performed. In order to render the distance function robust with respect to the partial occlusions, it is observed that if $\psi_i(S,T)$ is too much great, it does not supply useful information, cause of a possible occlusion. Then supposing useful only the informations provided by values of $\psi_i(S,T)$ ranging from 0 and $2 \cdot \overline{m}$ where $\overline{m}$ represents the average

$\overline{m} = \dfrac{1}{|S|} \cdot \displaystyle\sum_{i=1}^{|S|} \psi(S,T)$. A threshold operation that cuts only the values greater

than $2 \cdot \overline{m}$ is applied, leaving unchanged those smaller. That can be done with the following function:

$$\Delta(S,T) = \frac{1}{|\tilde{S}|}\sum_{i=1}^{|S|}\gamma_S^i \cdot \psi_i(S,T) + \frac{1}{|\tilde{T}|}\sum_{i=1}^{|T|}\gamma_T^i \cdot \psi_i(T,S) \tag{3}$$

where

$$\gamma_S^i = \frac{\left(S(i) - 2 \cdot E[S]\right) - \left|S(i) - 2 \cdot E[S]\right|}{2 \cdot \left(S(i) - 2 \cdot E[S]\right)}$$

$$\tilde{S} = \left\{(a_i, b_i) \in S \ni \gamma_S^i \neq 0\right\}$$

4. Experimental Results

There are several standard databases used by the scientific community in order to assess the performances of the proposed algorithms in the field of the face authentication. Two of the most used face databases are FERET [4] and AR Faces [3], while recognition rate and CMS (Cumulative Match Score) have been used as a measure of the performances (the CMS measure has been defined in details in the FERET protocol [4]). There are two main aspects to be investigated evaluating performances in case of occluded faces. The first one is to estimate the contribution of each face element to the global recognition rate.

It make sense that eyes, nose and mouth have different weights in the recognition task, so that occluding mouth the loss of information is minor than occluding the eyes. For this reason experiments have been conducted in order to evaluate the *degradation* of the recognition rate when at least one element of the face is occluded. The test as been done on a subset of *50* subjects from the AR Faces database. Three images have been used with different facial expression: neutral, angry and smile. In the first case only one eye has been occluded in all three images, used as probe set, while non-occluded faces in neutral condition compose the gallery set. In Figure 3 (a) are shown results in terms of CMS when the rank increases from *1* to *30*. For neutral images also when one of the eyes is occluded the CMS is *100*% just for rank *1*, while it drop dawn of about *25-30*% for the angry and smile images, because changes in expression introduce a further distortion in the resulting feature vector. In Figure 3 (b) is shown the case, in which both the eyes are occluded. The situation is almost the same for the neutral expression, while at rank *1* the CMS slow down to *50-65*% for smile and angry. This means that eyes by itselves provide almost the half of the information needed for recognition. In other words the contribution of the mouth and nose is less significant than that of the eyes, as confirmed also by Figure 3 (c), in which the mouth has been occluded. It can also be observed that for the smiling images the CMS at rank *1* is higher than for all other types of occlusions, it is because a smiling expression can be just considered as an occlusion, which is amounted to the mouth occlusion in this case. At last Figure 3 (d) shows that also when the nose is occluded a noticeable degradation of the CMS occurs for angry and smiling expression. An interpretation can be that the nose is almost invariant when facial expression changes occur, then occluding nose the recognition task becomes slightly harder. The second interesting aspect to be investigated consists in evaluating how good are the recognition performances when the dimensions of the occluded area increase. In order to test the robustness of ROF in this sense, the same subset of the AR Face database used in the previous experiment has been taken. For each face the neutral expression is used for training the system in the gallery, while neutral, angry and smile images with synthetic occlusion are used for testing in the probe.

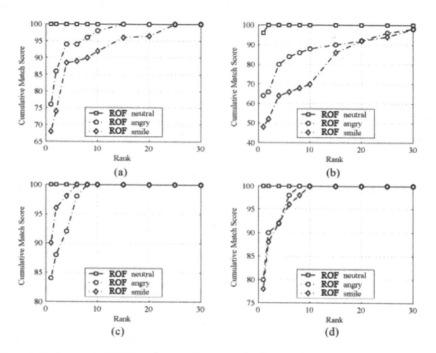

Figure 3. Performances of ROF on the neutral, angry and smile sets when one eye (a), both the eyes (b), the mouth (c) or the nose (d) are occluded.

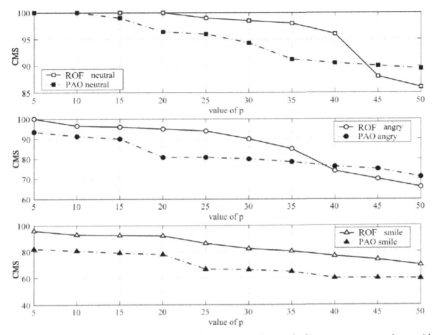

Figure 4. Performances of ROF when synthetic rectangular occlusion occurr, comparison with Martinez' algorithm.

Synthetic square occlusions of $p \times p$ dimension have been added, where p varies from a low of *5* to a maximum of *50*. For each value of p the square is randomly localized in the image *100* times and mean results are reported in Figure 4 (a), (b) and (c). For this experiment the performances of ROF have been compared with results obtained in analogous conditions by a probabilistic approach proposed by Martinez [172], referred as PAO, in this chapter. The PAO approach divides the face region in six elliptical regions, while ROF extracts from the original image only four rectangular zones. A less number of independent regions means that an higher robustness of the method is required because occlusions can affect more regions simultaneously. Figure 4 shows also drops of *10%* in the CMS of the two methods confirming the robustness of ROF with respect to the synthetic occlusions.

5. Conclusions

The interest of researchers for face recognition is firmly increasing in last years, so that several solution have been proposed until today. However the most part of the recent methods deal only with change in expressions and in illumination conditions, not considering the case of synthetic and natural occlusions. In particular the literature about fractals applications in Face Recognition is very poor. For these reasons in this chapter a new fractal based approach, namely ROF, is proposed. It is shown how IFS transformations can be readapted in order to provide a good signature for face images, useful for the face recognition task. The indexing process has been localized and a new metric is provided in order to deal with partial occlusions. Experimental results show the robustness of ROF with respect to synthetic occlusions (black squares randomly localized on the image) and natural occlusions of such face elements (eyes, nose or mouth). Future works can address the problem of automatic and finer localization of the face objects (eyes, nose and mouth) and increasing robustness to changes in illumination conditions.

References

1. R. Distasi, M. Nappi, M. Tucci, *FIRE: Fractal Indexing with Robust Extensions for Image Databases*, IEEE Transactions on Image Processing, vol. 12, Issue: 3, pp. 373-384, March 2003.
2. A. M. Martìnez, *Recognizing Imprecisely Localized, Partially Occluded and Expression Variant Faces from a Single Sample per Class,* IEEE Transactions on Pattern Analysis and Machine Intelligence, vol. 24, no. 6, pp. 748-763, June 2002.
3. A. M. Martìnez, *The AR face database*, CVC Tech. Report, no. 24, (1998).
4. P. J. Phillips, H. Moon, S. Rizvi and P. Rauss, *The FERET evaluation methodology for facerecognition algorithms*, IEEE Transaction on Pattern Analysis and Machine Intelligence, vol. 22, no. 10, pp. 1090-1104, October 2000.
5. Riccio D., Nappi M., *Defering range/domain comparisons in fractal image compression* in Proceedings 12th International Conference on Image Analysis and Processing, vol. 1, pp. 412-417, September 2003.
6. W. Zhao, R. Chellapa, P. J. Phillips and A. RosenFeld, *Face Recognition: A Literature Survey*, in ACM Computing Surveys, vol. 35, no. 4, pp. 399-458, December 2003.

Printed in the United States
By Bookmasters